Start With You
How Badass Executives are Transforming Their Lives (and Businesses) in Just 12 Quarters

For Business Owners and CEOs

D1178712

Peter C. Fuller
Contributors

Dr. Renee Kennedy Edwards, psychologist
Kristina Perry, certified health and life coach

Special Thanks

Susan Fuller for encouraging me to write this book and spending many hours of her time editing it.

Nicholas Fuller for creating the front and back cover design.

Carmen Patel for being the "iron that sharpens iron" on core concepts and continually challenging me to "be clearer."

Vistage® Worldwide groups 4271, 4699 and 9304 for being the inspiration behind this 12 Quarter platform.

Ken Thieneman, Diana Stewart, Nancy Duarte, Tom Cronin, Curt Vander Meer and Jennifer Deare for agreeing to share their stories with the world.

Matthew Perry for creating the graphics that help explain core concepts.

Norman and Kathy Fuller for taking the time to proofread.

ISBN:
978-1-68564-289-1

Table of Contents

2

Other Titles Coming Soon in This Series

Start With You for Working Moms, by Kristina Perry
Start With You for College Students
Start With You for Men
Start With You for Families
Start With You for Entrepreneurs
Start With You for Executive Coaches
Start With You for Life Coaches
Start With You for Organizations and Corporations
Start With You for Sales Teams
Start With You for SAHMs (stay-at-home moms)

Resources
All the planning materials you'll find in the book are
available at www.petercfuller.net/start-with-you and
www.catipult.ai

Foreword, Leo Bottary

I met Peter Fuller at a Vistage Worldwide® event in
Indianapolis in June 2016. I may have been the featured
speaker that day, but I was the one who walked away with the
big "aha." iteI knew then he was onto something – something

that could make a real difference for today's leaders, not just personally or professionally, but with both.

Most people, even many leaders, appear to be looking for the silver bullet to happiness and success, as evidenced by the popularity of content that's based on providing purported game-changing tips. (You know, with titles like "Three Keys to a Better Life" or "Five Ways to Vault Your Career to New Heights.") These tips all should come with a warning label. They typically address symptoms rather than root causes, and rarely consider the underlying principles necessary for helping anyone change their behavior long-term. Peter's book bridges that gap and does so in a way that is neither complicated nor requires you to perform superhuman feats.

Runner's World magazine's Joe Henderson once wrote that being truly accomplished at anything doesn't require you to do what no one else can do; it asks instead that you do the things anyone can do, but typically don't.

Take the time to explore the power of living a fused life and you'll discover that, with Peter's help and the support of your peers, anyone can do it. It's why this book is so powerful.

Enjoy!

Leo Bottary
Adjunct Professor, Rutgers University; co-author, *The Power of Peers: How the Company You Keep Drives Leadership, Growth & Success*

Start with You

Curt Vander Meer is the CEO of Endangered Species Chocolate, a category leader in the organic chocolate industry. His brand is sold globally in Whole Foods, Kroger and many others stores.

Curt had two dreams: 1) to take the month of July off without interruption and 2) for his company – which gives 10 percent of its net profits back to charities that protect endangered species – to give 3x more money away in a single year than the company gave the previous year. Curt viewed these two goals as both hard to achieve and completely disassociated from each other.

I believe that there are millions of people around the world just like Curt whose hearts, minds and guts look much like the figure to the right. They have a passion for doing something, but the requirements of their business or job combine with financial and other pressures to create a negative tamping force on the aspirations and life goals that are trying to surface.

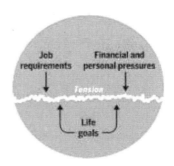

These opposing forces create tremendous tension that can manifest outwardly in anxiety, depression, irritability, apathy, resignation and even physical conditions like heart disease. Not surprisingly, heart disease is the number one killer in the world's capital of capitalism—the United States, according to the Centers for Disease Control and Prevention's website.

THE WESTERN PENDULUM

This tension is caused in part by what I call the Western Pendulum. The term *Western* is widely used to distinguish between capitalistic societies and their noncapitalistic counterparts around the world. While the term's etymology points to the geographic origination of modern capitalism in the United States, the term *Western* in this context no longer has geographic boundaries. It's merely used as an association with the work ethic and ideals that influence capitalistic cultures around the world.

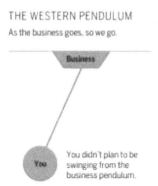

THE WESTERN PENDULUM

As the business goes, so we go.

Business

You

You didn't plan to be swinging from the business pendulum.

In these societies, work is considered the pivot point of life. Non-work related activities— what we call our "personal life"— take second priority to the work we feel we must do to provide an income to support a "nice life."

Many business owners and entrepreneurs stepped out on their own to balance and control the personal side of living. After just a short time, they found themselves on the wrong end of the pendulum, controlled by the very business that was supposed to give them more time and freedom to chase their passions. In some cases, where the business is the passion, the same still occurs.

Our personal life is swung back and forth, minute after minute, day after day, month after month and year after year in a seemingly directionless, random sway that almost insures against us achieving our dreams. One minute we're scheduled to be at our child's soccer game or school play and the next minute we're called back into the office for an "emergency" that takes us away from the life events we consider most important. Vacations are planned and then canceled. Even savings are drained to cover the salaries of employees we don't want to lose during a downturn.

It starts to feel like we are working for the business rather than the business working for us; that we are working in the business and not on it. The dreams we had when we started the business or career—like taking vacations or spending more time with family—often melt away into nothing but an impossible mirage. As the business swings us back and forth, the time we have on earth continues to wane.

Soon, we may feel like victims held hostage by a monster we created. We aren't victims, however, and likely didn't always have that mentality. We do have power, choices and a free will capable of changing our trajectory.

It's important to realize that one of the reasons our minds begin to frame the business activities we do (work) as things that must be done is rooted in the survival instinct that drives us to earn money to buy food, shelter and other items we need to live. Activities that don't immediately seem to impact survival are held in tension and incongruence with those that do. When this happens, our mind is creating an imbalance that may generate anxieties, frustrations and a false sense of being a victim.

In reality, there is nothing you must do, and you can become a victim of your perception in the way your situation occurs. Don't judge yourself, though. Most, if not all, humans embody this stress and viewpoint of their world and their power (or lack thereof) to change it.

"IF YOU DON'T DESIGN YOUR LIFE PLAN, THERE ARE CHANCES THAT YOU'LL FALL INTO SOMEONE ELSE'S PLAN. AND GUESS WHAT THEY HAVE SCHEDULED FOR YOU? NOT MUCH."—JIM ROHN, ENTREPRENEUR AND MOTIVATIONAL SPEAKER

Changing Your Position

This book can help you break free and reverse your position on the Western Pendulum to put you back in control of your life through a process that also grows your business at the same time.
Yes, both are possible to achieve.

THE BALANCED PENDULUM
Your desired outcomes drive the business

You

Business

Balance reduces stress and drives better business decisions.

The concepts presented in this book and 12-quarter process are proven to work, simple to execute and do not add to your workload. While the process is simple, the initial concept of fusing personal life and business may initially occur as counterintuitive to achieving success in either of those areas.

Curt, like many I coach, struggled at first to see how balance can grow the business.

ME: What is it you *want* in 12 quarters?

Curt: In my business?

Me: In your life; they are the same. What is it you *want*?

Curt: I've always wanted to take the month of July off with my family. But, I can't do that.

ME: Ok. Let's open your Outcome Statement with that: "The year is 2019 and I am spending the month of July with my family without interruption from the business."

Curt: I still don't see what vacation has to do with my business plan.

Me: What's stopping you from taking four weeks off *now?*

At this point, Curt paused and looked around the room at his peer board members and then back at me.

Curt: Ok. I think I get it. I can't take them now because I haven't developed my executive team to the level where I can leave the company for four weeks and know it will be fine. I've run a CEO-centric business.

Me: The year is 2019 and I'm taking the month of July off, uninterrupted, with my family. How are you going to make that happen?

Curt: I need to spend the next 12 quarters developing my management team.

Me: What else might happen when your management team is stronger?

Curt: Perhaps my revenue and profits would increase at a faster pace.

Me: The year is 2019 and I'm taking the month of July off, uninterrupted, with my family *and* my company's donations to fulfill its brand promise have increased 300 percent over 2016 levels.

Curt: I'll write it down.

Your Choice and Intention

To be rigorous, you need to acknowledge your complicity in the way your life is today and eliminate thoughts or language that may hint at a victim mentality. Yes, business owners and CEOs also have victim mentalities. This mindset generates the limiting beliefs that hold them back from using the control they have to transform not only their lives but also their leadership.

This book can help you use the control you already have by:

- ***Identifying what is important to you.*** *This book doesn't preach what "is" a balanced life. That definition is entirely up to you. Rather, it helps you identify your priorities and then place them in the balance of the other activities you need to accomplish.*

- ***Building a plan made of choice you will commit to making based on your priorities.*** *I call this "bending the business around your will."*

- ***Working the plan over the course of 12 quarters.*** *Transformation doesn't happen overnight, and, in most cases, it doesn't happen by simply doing what someone else tells you to do. Transformation, through this book, comes from within you, gradually, as you are building the life you want to live 12 quarters from now.*

- ***Providing a system of online resources, coaches and accountability partners*** *that can help you keep the commitments you'll make to yourself on your plan. At LiveFused.com, you'll find the material and tools covered here, plus a world of peers and coaches who are working toward their visions and eager to help you achieve yours.*

By the end of the 12 quarters, your position on the pendulum could be reversed, and you'll be living a transformed life that may include multiple 12-quarter sprints. Life may be a marathon, but our minds can only grasp and manage short distances at one time, hence the business application of the word "sprint." You'll be focusing on 12 quarters; that's only three years. In 12 quarters, you won't be a servant of the business or your job. It will be serving you.

"The process lets you pick who you want to become or accelerate who you already are. It's a life accelerator," said

Ken Thieneman, CEO of Thieneman Construction, Inc. in Indianapolis, IN. "Instead of feeling like you have to do life, the 12-quarter process changed the way life occurred to me and empowered me to take 100 percent control of my life—with no excuses. And then drive, each day, to make it happen."

Your Acceleration Platform to Living a Fused Life

We'll learn more about Ken's experience later, but what he is describing is what I call Fused Living. He's combined life, business and an ecosystem of peers into one single, strategic plan that is fused together by the intentions of his purpose. Living fused isn't how we normally do things. We like to keep many lives— business, personal and community—separate. But that limits our power to move forward toward our goals and desires.

What you'll experience through this book is the gradual fusing of the different aspects of your life into one single timeline of deliberate choices you'll plan to make.

To do that, you'll need this platform.

A platform is something upon which other things can rest or, in technology, other technologies can be developed upon. That's what this book is: a platform for your intentions to be realized and managed within one context— you. You can place programs for weight loss, meditation, professional growth, life coaching, executive coaching and business growth and anything else on this platform, if those

programs will exist within the intention you'll set for the way your life will be 12
quarters from now.

Losing weight, for instance, may be a thing you want to do. If, however, you are choosing to lose weight because in 12 quarters you plan to purchase a condo on the beach, reduce your time in the office by one full day and be healthy enough to enjoy an active lifestyle with friends, then you are more likely to accomplish the task of losing weight. You're going to give yourself 12 quarters to be at your desired weight, thus eliminating the stress caused by intention-less efforts to drop weight quickly which usually result in weight gain after the short-term diet program ends.

As a platform for your life, this is not a tactical program that directs your activities. You direct your activities to achieve your desired results. If you have an executive or life coach (and I recommend that every executive have one), this platform will not compete with their coaching, but rather enhance it. Good coaches explore your life experiences and help you transform or navigate through them. That expertise, when applied to your 12-quarter plan, becomes even more valuable. It's like adding rocket fuel to your tank.

Concepts You'll Learn

I've helped start more than a dozen companies, two industry associations, and one non-profit, and have coached dozens of business owners, CEOs, executives and mid-level managers and employees. Through that experience, I learned something about myself that is continually reflected in the lives of those with whom I work: plans and strategies often fail not because the plan was wrong, but rather because I didn't make the necessary adjustments to my world view to driving the success I expected.

To fully transform into living a fused life, we must alter the way we think. That's not easy to do. In fact, it is almost impossible to do by just reading. Humans understand best when concepts are experienced, not just taught.

To that end, you're going to learn some paramount new realities and then knead these ideas into a plan of action that you will live. Gradually, as you live the plan, your mind will shift to a new way of thinking.

Here are a few of the key concepts I cover:

1. Beliefs: how they can limit your performance.
2. Judgment: how to transform your view of situations.
3. Language: how language changes everything.

"OUR GOALS CAN ONLY BE REACHED THROUGH A VEHICLE OF A PLAN, IN WHICH WE MUST FERVENTLY BELIEVE, AND UPON WHICH WE MUST VIGOROUSLY ACT. THERE IS NO OTHER ROUTE TO SUCCESS."—PABLO PICASSO

First, we'll explore how we think, learn and react so you can actively identify and clear beliefs you may currently hold that will limit your progress toward your goal.

Second, you'll transform how situations occur to you. Your mind is a very biased machine, affected by everyone and every situation it experiences. Becoming aware of this will help transform your leadership and ability to navigate the inevitable challenges you'll face while creating your 12-quarter outcome.

Finally, we'll begin the 12-quarter process of fusing your business, personal, professional and community lives into one intentional and highly active strategic plan.

Resources

All the steps and planning tools in this book are available at livefused.com. There, you will also find an online community of business owners, CEOs, executives, coaches and others with whom you can partner for accountability or even tap into services that may help you execute your plan more quickly.

I hope you check it out and join!

Now, let's get moving on your 12 quarters. Time, after all, is waiting for you to finish reading this book.

How You Think, Learn & React

The human brain is a mysteriously wonderful machine about which we know relatively nothing. Governments are just now beginning to direct billions of dollars into understanding the gray matter than controls every bodily function, drives every thought and creates actions that shape and destroy the lives of others.

I'm no scientist, but my experiences both personally and as an executive coach have confirmed what religion and philosophy have said for thousands of years: to change ourselves, we must transform our language which changes our thoughts, which, when tested by experiences, renews and transforms our beliefs.

Let's look first at the biology of language and then at experiences.

The Biology of Language

One of the most interesting theories in transformational science is Nero-Linguistic Programming (NLP). Pioneered by psychotherapists Richard Bandler and John Grinder, NLP is a methodology that models techniques from psychotherapists Virginia Satir, Milton Erickson and Fritz Perls, the founder of Gestalt therapy. The idea behind NLP was to model, through language, transformation for the client. Some early practitioners used hypnosis and claimed to be able to break people of various habits like smoking and drinking. NLP has also been widely utilized in goal-setting programs designed to change the way we act by changing the way we think of ourselves.

Discoveries in the field of listening complement assumptions NLP theorists have been making for 40 years—that the brain uses deeply held beliefs to frame its world of interactions. Change the beliefs and the actions taken will be altered and different outcomes will be achieved.

Jerker Rönnberg developed a model for listening, called the Ease of Language Understanding (ELU). Rönnberg is a professor of psychology at Linköping University in Sweden. His model builds on the assumption that the brain "rapidly, automatically, and multi-modally binds phonological" information together and represents it in a very short-term buffer. When hearing is impaired, our brains fill in missing information based, to a certain extent, upon our inherent biases or beliefs.

Our hearing is always impaired. Our thoughts, judgments and environmental distractions reduce listening and the information we consciously absorb. When our brains fill in the gaps between what we hear and absorb with our stored beliefs, "semantic framing," as Rönnberg calls it, is induced.

In other words, our brains use stored data to fill in missing information and create beliefs about what we are experiencing. That stored data is a well of beliefs. If it sounds circular, it's because it is circular. Let's say you're at a party and speaking to someone with an accent that sounds British. You may never ask the person where they are from, but the next day you may declare to a colleague that you had a pleasant conversation with an Englishman at the party. Your brain heard an accent, compared it with its database of beliefs about similar sounding voices and their geographical origin and then created a story about the chance encounter that may or may not be true.

This cycle of listening, filling in data and creating stories is why, physiologically speaking, humans are incapable of understanding the truth.

Beliefs are the well of information from which the brain draws information to complete the puzzle. When, through language, new ideas are absorbed, they need to be put into action and experienced for them to become beliefs. Once believed, the water in our well of data is transformed, and our brains will then interpret situations much differently.

In the case of the encounter with the alleged British accent, if the belief were that all accents are unknown until clearly defined by the person with the accent, then the resulting belief would have been that a conversation occurred with a nice person with an accent. The action taken may have been to discover the truth by asking the person about his or her place of origin.

Why is this important?

You have a well of beliefs and biases that have been filled through years of interactions and influences. Some of them are true, and some of them are limiting. Many are bound to emotions, both positive and negative. To reach your 12-quarter personal and business goals, you're going to be asked to think bigger than perhaps you ever have in the past. I'm going to stretch you to look beyond what you think you can achieve based on your past performance, and to break from the past and begin to build what you want to create. The space between what you believe can be achieved and what you want to create for yourself is filled with beliefs and biases—usually about why you can't possibly build the outcome you desire.

Because the clear majority of our understanding comes from language (verbal and body) and because our physiology makes it impossible to know the truth, we're going to spend a lot of time talking about language, limiting beliefs, perceptions and how those you have permeate your life without you even knowing it. Once you become mindful of that which is limiting and begin to change your tape through language, you'll start to achieve the outcome you truly desire.

Another way of understanding the power of thought is through the perspective of Rational Emotive Behavior Therapy (REBT), a therapeutic approach developed by Dr. Albert Ellis in 1955. This framework integrates emotions, behavior and cognitions as an interdependent process. It emphasizes that people's views, often accompanied by rigid and extreme thinking, contribute to their stressful feelings, thoughts and actions.

This irrational thinking can limit individuals' levels of achievement while taking them down a path of selflimiting behavior. Mary, a junior architect at a prestigious firm, had been asked to share her creative design with a high-end client in a formal presentation the following week. Prone to anxiousness (anxiety?) and self-deprecating thoughts, Mary believed she was asked to do this as a default, given that presentations typically include a minimum of three different designs for the client to choose from. Mary

reasoned that the other two architects had more successful designs and that hers was simply included to show up the others being offered. During the week, Mary continued to think negatively about her upcoming presentation, and as a result, she experienced severe insomnia and high anxiety. She tried to calm herself by feeding her cravings for carbohydrates
while drinking wine almost every night to help her relax. By the time of the client presentation, Mary was exhausted and felt depressed. Her delivery was flat and disappointing. Not surprisingly, the client chose her peer's design over hers just as she had imagined.

This example shows the strong relationship among Mary's beliefs (thoughts), feelings and actions. While Mary was chosen to present her design because of her high creativity and excellent skillset, her rigid and irrational beliefs about herself stressed her out and took her down a path of self-sabotaging behavior that resulted in her expected result: failure. This destructive path reinforces Mary's limiting belief system and therefore helps keep it alive when the next opportunity arises.

Mary's experience demonstrates the power of one's mind and how it can directly impact one's mood, behavior and results. Rational Emotive Behavior Therapy (REBT) focuses on changing one's irrational beliefs to more rational ways of thinking and processing one's world. By disputing irrational thought, a person can challenge his or her way of viewing the world while in turn, reducing the overall stress and disturbance that result from dysfunctional thinking. This involves challenging the current thought process by asking, "Where is the rational evidence for or against this belief?" In addition, asking, "What are some rational alternative responses to this belief?" can help open other modes of thought.

Understanding where irrational thoughts derive from can assist awareness into a more rational and logical way of viewing and reacting to the world. The most important aspect to REBT is that it is not the things that cause one mental distress, rather it is simply how one perceives these things. By changing a person's current thought process into a more rational alternative, one may feel and behave more rationally which may in turn offer more positive results.

In addition, REBT helps reduce absolutist thought processing that is often accompanied by "all or none" thinking with common language such as, "I should" and "I must" that result in rigid views of oneself and of the world. Offering up alternative responses that incorporate more flexible thinking, a person learns to be more accepting and less judgmental in the process.[1]

Experiences and Intention

Any action we take or observe and the consequent result fall broadly into the definition of the word *experience*. Experience is the ingredient that transforms the

1
  Dryden, W. & Neenan, M. (2004). The rational emotive behavioural approach to therapeutic change. Thousand Oaks, CA: SAGE Publications, Inc.

Mahoney, M. (Ed). (1995). Cognitive and constructive psychotherapies theory, research, & practice. New York, NY: Springer Publishing Company

Mulhauser, G. (n.d.). An introduction to Rational Emotive Behaviour Therapy. Retrieved from http://counsellingresource.com/therapy/types/rational-emotive/

knowledge you hear, read and observe into beliefs and biases. As the famous Roman Ruler, Julius Caesar once wrote, "Experience is the teacher of all things."

This book presents concepts with a system to help you experience those truths *while* you work to reverse your position on the pendulum. I don't expect you to fully believe or absorb everything you'll read here the first time you read it.

These ideas tend to come to life through the actions you will take and the results you'll achieve. Once you experience the concepts in this book working in conjunction with your plan, you may begin to believe them within your own context. This book isn't prescriptive, in other words. You won't be told exactly what to do or think. You'll be guided into experiencing concepts and make them uniquely yours as you progress along your journey to create the life you want to live and business you want to lead.

By the end of the 12 quarters, you will be able to achieve goals you once thought were impossible while also transforming your leadership skills (at home and in the office) in the process.

Every Experience is Unique

Experiences are uniquely interpreted by your biology, past and present social environments and beliefs already formed. Experiences often serve to prove or disprove the beliefs we hold dear. Everyone's experience is different because each human being is unique. The way we interpret experiences, therefore, is as unique as we are.

Because you are unique, there can be no pre-defined set of experiences that I or anyone else can recommend that will transform your life and business into what you wish it to become in 12 quarters. Other programs or books that tell you what actions to take without taking into consideration the experience you are having are simply pulling tactics that worked for someone else out of their context and expecting them to work for you, within your context. The result is predictable: actions are taken for a time and then set aside because their relevance to an individual's life context wanes quickly. Experiences within your context are part of the solution.

Intention Changes Language and Drives Your Experiences

The key ingredient that this platform helps you generate is the intention. Webster's Dictionary defines intention as "the thing you plan to do or achieve." It's much more than that, however.

Deepak Chopra, M.D., is a leader in integrative medicine and founder of the Chopra Center. He defines intention as: "a directed impulse of consciousness that contains the seed form of that which you aim to create. Like real seeds, intentions can't grow if you hold on to them. Only when you release your intentions into the fertile depths of your consciousness can they grow and flourish."

Your intention may not be known now, but don't worry, that's what the exercises in this book will help you discern. It's in there—deep inside you or at the surface— that longing, purpose or mission you want to accomplish or that life you want to live. Stretch yourself; be yourself. Don't hold back as you walk through the lessons here. Holding back only hurts yourself. This is your journey. Make it big.

YOU ONLY HAVE ONE LIFE TO LIVE AN ENTIRE LIFE TO LOSE.

Your Intention, Not Mine

Earlier we discussed the purpose everyone has, and how this book will help align this purpose with your business objectives, thus allowing both to not only exist together but also be realized with the reality you'll craft for yourself.

That purpose is going to fuel the intention you'll define, the strategic plan you're going to build. Think of it this way— intention is the objective you're trying to achieve; only it is bigger and more expensive than most objectives placed into a typical strategic plan because this intention is going to meld your business and personal lives into one single strand of time from which you operate and will use to create your outcome. It is like Chopra said—a directed impulse of your consciousness that will grow into the world you believe is possible.

As Alvin Toffler, a writer and futurist, once wrote: "You've got to think about big things while you are doing small things so that all the small things go in the right direction."

The intention is the big plan—the place you will arrive in 12 quarters. To get there, you'll accomplish many small and many large tasks and strategies, which will be your experience, guided by your intention.

Within the context of your experience, guided by your intention, you'll live the concepts we'll cover in this book. While experiencing them within your context and while building your plans, your mind will interpret them in a way that is unique and relevant to you. Old beliefs about business or life may fall away, transform or become more meaningful. Whatever your experience, it will be yours, and you will transform yourself, your leadership, your business and your life over 12 quarters
if you stick to the plan.

YOU WON'T FIND A PROCESS TO TRANSFORM WITHIN THESE PAGES. INSTEAD, YOU'LL FIND A PLATFORM FOR BUILDING AND EXPERIENCING YOUR OWN TRANSFORMATION.

Identify & Remove Limiting Beliefs

"DON'T BE INTIMIDATED BY WHAT YOU DON'T KNOW. THAT CAN BE YOUR GREATEST STRENGTH AND ENSURE THAT YOU DO THINGS DIFFERENTLY FROM EVERYONE ELSE." –SARA BLAKELY, FOUNDER OF SPANX

There's something inside you that's bugging you. Maybe you know what it is; maybe you don't. You just have this feeling that something isn't quite the way it could be.

It's okay. You're okay. No one who ever did anything with their life escaped the feeling you have inside you right now. No one. What do I mean by "do anything with their life?" Nothing. I don't mean anything because I don't know everyone on the planet and am certainly not aware of their definition of doing "something." And that means I don't know your definition of "something." I don't know what is in your mind. I don't know the emotions that drove you to pick up this book or that drive you to explore what may be a new phase in your life.

Doing "something" with your life is up to you to define. No one else. Just you. If you know what that "something" is that you want to do and you don't at least give it a shot, you are going to be your harshest critic. The first step forward in our path to living a fused life is to identify and remove the limiting beliefs that may be holding us back from doing what we know we should try.

Interjections and Biases

There are two primary types of limiting beliefs: 1) an interjection and 2) bias.

An interjection is a term coined by Fritz Perls, the founder of Gestalt therapy. An interjection is an idea imposed upon us by society, religion, parents, peers and our environment. Interjections become limiting beliefs that our mind can perceive as actionable truth. Bias is simply anything you currently think to be true that limits the options you perceive to exist and, consequently, the actions you take. Both interjections and biases fall under the broad umbrella category of *limiting belief.*

Another way to think about limiting beliefs is to picture a horse wearing blinders. These black leather squares are placed to the sides of the horse's eyes to block its peripheral vision. The horse can only see what is directly in front of it, thus reducing the possibilities for action it perceives to only those presented by the immediate situation. Blinders are perfect for horse racing because they force the horse to rely on the jockey for all strategic decisions and prevent it from being swayed by distractions.

You don't have a jockey, however, to guide your decisions and frame the field of play. But you do have blinders on, and they severely restrict the options you perceive to exist.

Most of us—myself included—don't think we have limiting beliefs because they are beliefs. And that's the fundamental problem. If we believe something is true, then we don't perceive it as limiting our actions but rather guiding them. We see what is in front of us and not the blinders, in other words.

Most limiting beliefs first occur with the word "should" or "could" in front of them. Here are a few examples you may have heard:

- You should eat all the food on your plate because people are starving.
- You should hold a steady job because it is too risky to start your own business.
- You shouldn't quit your job to rear your children.
- You should start your own business and stop working for the man.
- You should vacation at Disney World.
- You should have kids.
- You should get married.
- You shouldn't get divorced.
- You should travel more.
- You should go to this church on this block.
- You should live in this suburb.
- You shouldn't confront your boss.
- You shouldn't ask for a raise.
- You shouldn't file sexual harassment charges because you might lose your job.
- You could be more successful if only you had an MBA.

- You could have lived elsewhere, but you didn't get your paperwork into the office on time.

- I shouldn't fire this employee because he's been with me for a long time.

- I shouldn't try to transition to a new career because it's too risky.

- You could make a lot more money if you switch jobs.

- You could be better off if you were smarter.

Limiting beliefs also disguise themselves as facts.

- You are supposed to have children when married.

- A woman cannot make as much money as a man.

- A man needs to provide for his family.

- The world is flat.

- People will never travel at the speed of sound.

- People will never travel at the speed of light.

- World hunger will never be solved.

- My business will never be a $100 million enterprise.

- I am stuck in my career because I am the breadwinner.

- I am disadvantaged as a woman in a man's world.

- I'm disadvantaged as a minority.

29

- A black woman can never become the first female engineer at NASA.
- NASA would never place a black woman in charge of a brand-new IBM computer.
- A black woman would never be awarded the Presidential Medal of Freedom and have a research facility named in her honor.

Let's spend a minute on the last three bullet points. They come from the fantastic, must-see movie called *Hidden Figures*, directed by Theodore Melfi, based on the sametitled non-fiction book by Margot Lee Shetterly.

This remarkable film chronicles the lives of three African-American female mathematicians in the 1960s. All three worked for NASA in Virginia and were part of the segregated West Area Computers division of the Langley Research Center. Back then, computers referred to human beings, not machines. These women were "computers" that various divisions of NASA would call upon to help with calculations.

Katherine Johnson calculated the trajectories for the Apollo 11, Apollo 13 and many space shuttle missions. Later, she was awarded the Presidential Medal of Freedom and a facility was named in her honor.

The awards came not just because of her brilliance. Many people at NASA (if not all of them) are incredibly brilliant. She was honored, in part, for the extreme fortitude she maintained during a tumultuous, segregated time in

American history that stacked the cards of opportunity against her in every way. Not only did she persevere through discrimination, her attitude and grace helped transform NASA into an institution of greater opportunity for all races, ahead of many other institutions in the United States at that time.

Mary Jackson, a friend of Goble's, became the first black female engineer in NASA, having to fight a segregated education system in court just to get the same access to education others had.

Dorothy Vaughan seized upon an opportunity to save the women of the West Area Computers from being replaced by a new IBM 7090. Realizing few at NASA knew how to run the complex, massive machine, she taught herself Fortran, a computer language used to program the IBM by "borrowing" a book from a whitesonly library that she was forcefully removed from by security. She then taught all the woman who worked with her and became the only group in Langley who could run the machine. Jobs were saved, and she became the supervisor of the new computing division.

These three women undoubtedly confronted intrinsic and extrinsic biases and interjections. Rather than believing them to be true and allowing them to limit their actions, they chose to believe that the impossible was, in fact, possible.

Their actions reshaped the way African-American women occurred to NASA executives. It didn't happen overnight. Their transformation came as they experienced minor victories and began to believe more fully in the possibility that they could continue to change their world and shape it to the outcome they, not others, desired. The more success they experienced, the less power limiting beliefs held over their lives. As they transformed, those around them did also.

As a leader, it is important to remember that you won't transform alone. Your victories are shared. As your beliefs about what is possible change, so will the beliefs of those you lead.

As these three women—and millions of others throughout history just like them demonstrated— transformation of self happens contemporaneously with the transformation of others.

As the narrator of *Start Trek* proclaimed at the beginning of every episode, "boldly go where no one has gone before."

Here's a brief exercise. Take a moment to jot down answers to these questions with whatever comes to mind.

- What are your limiting beliefs? Remember, a limiting belief will not occur as limiting. It will occur as truth.
- What occurs as true about your business or job?
- What occurs as true about your time outside of your business?
- What occurs as true about yourself?

Is what occurs true or could there be a different truth that someone else may hold?

Case Study, Jennifer Deare of D3-NYC

Jennifer Deare is one of my clients and a very successful executive in the capital of marketing and advertising, New York City. With more than 30 years in the industry, Jennifer has weathered many storms, beaten dozens of competitors and thrived in an industry known to be littered with others who just could not compete in her fast-paced world. She's the least likely person you'd expect to be hampered by limiting beliefs.

With Jennifer's permission, I'm sharing her list.

- I should be more productive.
- I should have gotten more done this week; it is already Wednesday, and I haven't made any new business calls.
- I should have watched the cash flow more.
- I should have been more decisive.
- I should stop drinking.
- I should stop picking at myself.
- I should have returned the stuff to Athleta®.
- I should have saved more money already.
- I should have seen my sister before she left.
- I am not pretty anymore.
- I am not motivated anymore.
- I am not sexy anymore.
- I am not funny anymore.

- I am not a good friend anymore.
- I am not a good sister anymore.
- I am not trying hard enough.
- I am not a good therapy patient.
- I am not paying enough attention to Chris.
- I am not generous.
- I am not a good leader.
- I am not fun to be around.
- I am not smart enough.
- I am not focused.
- I am not a planner.
- I am not a true entrepreneur.
- I am a pest to my kid and husband (and at work).
- I am a nut.
- I am tired.
- I am a joke.
- I am a phony.
- I am a loser.
- I am not honest.
- I am worn out.
- I am burnt out.
- I am lazy.
- I am crazy.
- I am frustrated.
- I am bored.
- I am lost.
- I am going through the motions.

Everything above bombards Jennifer daily. Despite her success as a woman-owned business in a cut-throat world, her mind still bombards her with beliefs that are false.

Jennifer's assignment was to begin writing down truths that counter each one of those beliefs. Here are two of her counters that she offered to share.

I am not productive
Yes, I am very productive. Last night I took a client out to dinner for several hours even thought I had gotten up at 4:45 AM yesterday, and today I got up early, met a client early this AM to discuss business, have arranged to go with her to an event tonight and during the day I have a couple of meetings that I added into my schedule. I've already done a short review (30 minutes) with my junior partners and am working on my 20 minutes [of meditation], having meditated for seven minutes on the train this AM.

I'm supposed to know all the answers
This morning I comfortably admitted that I was stumped for a reply with a client but that I wanted to help any way I could. I am practicing asking questions and putting less pressure on myself to be the answer girl.

Both limiting beliefs were affecting her ability to be a transformational leader. Her drive to know all the answers kept her from being able to meditate for just 20 minutes every day, a key component of transformation that I'll discuss later in the book. As she tried to quiet her mind, her belief that she must know everything compelled her to break from her quiet mind to pick up her phone and check the latest industry trade rags.

The idea that she isn't productive hampered her ability to spend time thinking strategically, as productivity was defined by getting things done. Strategic thinking isn't a task-driven exercise and doing it usually doesn't result in the immediate gratification of checking boxes off a list.

When she—or any of us—believe we aren't something, we will act under that stress in a subconscious attempt to disprove ourselves. We'll never win.

We need to change the stories we tell ourselves. And that starts by not allowing our minds to cram false ideas about ourselves into our thought streams. It will take discipline to do this and, of course, mindfulness, which is necessary to make the right choices.

CHOICE—THE POWER BEHIND THE UNIVERSE

According to scientific theory, the universe began as a stupendous array of light and energy that exploded 13.7 billion (or so) years ago. Science isn't sure what caused the explosion of nothing into something, but many theologies point to a supernatural intelligence that chose to create a universe different from the one it originally occupied (and may still occupy, depending on your belief system) and then took the action of the Big Bang to bring about its will.

You, too, have the power to choose to take responsibility for your life and, as the Creator did years ago, create your alternate universe. An alternate universe is anything that's different from the life you are currently living. If you don't like what you are doing now or where you are living, you have the choice to change into a different occupation or place of residence. Your limiting beliefs may tell you otherwise, however, and attempt to turn you into a victim, but the truth is that choice is the ultimate power you have.

If you're a business owner, you may love the business you started and hate the life the business is forcing you to live. Or, you could love both and have a burning desire to start something different—to give back in some way. That desire is going to weigh on you—until you make a choice.

If your desire is to maintain your status quo and do nothing differently, choosing not to change is, in fact, a choice to preserve. Those who take that path are choosing to act to maintain their current status quo. And that's okay; if you love where you are. Choosing to keep the current situation requires the same intention as wanting to change it. I've coached people who love their lives but still decided to use the tools in this book to intentionally preserve the life they lived from distractions and opportunities that often arise.

LIMITING BELIEFS BECOME STORIES

The irony of human development is that the brain frames events and experiences early in our childhood when we don't have the capacity to adequately understand what we are framing. A mental frame is a construct by which and through which we view the world.

For example, if a parent routinely tells their child that they will never succeed in life, then the child's mind may create a frame of themselves as a failure. Once firmly established by repeated comments (interjections) and experience failing to meet the parents' expectations, that mental frame may become a limiting belief that generates a life-long story: "I am a failure and therefore anything I try will fail."

Once believed as truth, future opportunities the child may encounter as an adult might be viewed and evaluated based on the story that failure is a likely outcome of trying. The resulting action may be to simply not plan in the first place. The same could be true positive reinforcement during childhood. Tell a child they're a prince or princess early on and some children will believe it—and may act like a spoiled brat for the rest of their life.

The mental frame, formed by limiting beliefs, creates stories about ourselves and our world. These stories are powerful and incredibly dangerous tools used routinely by our minds. In fact, as we learned earlier in the previous chapter, our mind taps the well of these stories and beliefs to fill in missing information and generate our truth to what we see and experience.

Here's another example:

Let's say you've had numerous experiences with employees who would sneak out of your building to use illegal drugs. After several years of this experience, your mind puts meaning to the event of employees leaving your building during work hours. It occurs to you that they are leaving to do drugs.

In reality, the event of an employee leaving the building during work hours means nothing. Patterns of similar events in the past associated with former employees aren't attributable to other employees in the present. If you act against a new employee who just happened to behave in the manor consistent with your mind's frame for the story that "drug abuse" is occurring, you may be compelled to take actions against the employee that aren't justified.

Stories, in other words, are dangerous. They may not be true, and they may be stopping you from building the life and business you truly desire to have in 12 quarters.

Up next are three of the top stories I've coached people through. While you're reading them, think of your own stories.

STORY 1: I DON'T HAVE TIME TO FOCUS ON MY PERSONAL AMBITIONS.

No one owns time or has it. We do, however, make time. Time is attached to the physical world. It is the universal force of measurement that gradually drives all substances into a different form of existence. Time is running you into the ground.

We never know when we will expire, but expire we will. That's a fact. The story in your head that you don't have time for your personal ambitions is only true if you continue to operate as if that is truth. Doing so results in inaction that only reinforces the story.

Anyone can wake up 10 minutes earlier each day or go to sleep 10 minutes later. Time can be made if the choice is made to make time.

STORY 2: I DON'T HAVE THE RESOURCES TO FOLLOW MY AMBITION.

For those of us who live on planet Earth, this story is just an excuse. Earth has all the resources we need to accomplish any ambition. Finding them, however, takes work and time. Convincing the caretakers of those resources to let us use them also takes time (and thick skin that can stand rejection).

The truth, however, is that you do have access to the resources you need to follow your ambition. You just need to find them.

STORY 3: I DON'T HAVE THE KNOWLEDGE OR SKILLS NECESSARY TO ACHIEVE MY GOAL.

This is just another excuse that prevents us from taking the first action necessary to secure the knowledge needed. Programs, degrees, certifications and training exist for virtually anything we want to do. We can get the training if we choose to do so.

Usually, this excuse has roots in deeper truths that must be confronted. Among them are 1) comfort with the status quo and 2) fear of losing a current job that provides security.

What are some of the stories in your head? Take a moment and list them on a sheet of paper. Consider:

- What stories am I telling myself about my business that are just excuses?
- What stories am I telling myself about my finances?
- What stories am I telling myself about taking time off?
- What stories am I telling myself about my skills and education?

DON'T READ FURTHER

To continue with this book, you need to make a choice now. That choice is to disown the *interjections* and *biases* you have in your mind that are creating *limiting beliefs* that lead to *stories* about yourself and others that may not be true.

Whatever they are, toss them. All of them. Do you hear your father telling you that you are worthless? Trash that interjection. Are you making millions and think you have "no time for the family?" Flush it. Are you a mother in middle management who thinks that she can't possibly earn a decent income and spend the time she wants with her children? Abandon that belief right now.

It is important to observe, analyze and surrender these thoughts for transformation to occur. To not maintain careful vigilance over your stories is to possibly practice avoidance, which will only continue to hamper your ability to drive forward unencumbered toward your goals.

Transform Your View of Events

One of my favorite books is *The Three Laws of Performance* by Steve Zaffron and Dave Logan. I coach the laws in this book regularly to my clients. The book covers three laws that are immutable in business and life because they are true to the way human beings experience events.

The first law of performance: How people perform correlates to how situations *occur* to them.[1]

The word "occurs" here is telling. Notice the authors didn't say "the way situations are." The reason for this important word choice is attached to what we covered previously about stories, limiting beliefs and framings. We don't know how a situation is. All we have to go by is how it occurs to us as framed by the stories, biases and interjections in our mind. How situations occur to us is likely different than how they occur to others. Since situations occur based on biases and stories that, if we are mindful, we can identify as not true, then it is possible to change the way a situation occurs to us and then also change the actions we would take, thus opening us up to a world of previously shuttered possibilities.

---

[1] Steve Zaffron and David Logan, *The Three Laws of Performance*: *Rewriting the Future of Your Organization and Your Life*. ((San Francisco: Josse Bass, 2009), 6.

To live a fused life and achieve greater balance, we're going to have to change the way situations occur to us.

Remember the Western Pendulum? It exists primarily because our lives occur as bifurcated between personal and business. When it occurs as two separate lives, we act as if they are separate and the result we achieve is the imbalance of working for the business rather than it working for us.

"MY PHILOSOPHY OF LIFE IS THAT IF WE MAKE UP OUR MIND WHAT WE ARE GOING TO MAKE OF OUR LIVES, THEN WORK HARD TOWARD THAT GOAL, WE NEVER LOSE— SOMEHOW WE ALWAYS WIN OUT." —RONALD REAGAN

TRANSFORMATION 1: THERE IS NO DISTINCTION BETWEEN BUSINESS LIFE AND PERSONAL LIFE.

Understanding that there is no distinction between self and business is something that confounds the wisest masters of business among us.

It confounded me, too, when I was building my companies. In fact, I never gave it much thought. The business had needs, and my "self" had needs. The two were distinguished in my mind and therefore manifested as completely disconnected from each other in my visible life.

Occurs   Belief   Action   Result

43

Because business and life occurred that way, I had certain self-limiting beliefs that were more than just ideas. Here are just a few of the ones I had in my mind:

- Don't bring your personal issues into work.
- The business comes first because it provides the income needed to sustain you.
- The hardest workers are connected 24/7.
- To be successful as an entrepreneur, you have to give all to your business.
- If you're not on all the time, someone else will be.
- Sacrifice for the business, and you'll get a huge payout that will allow you to take time off and enjoy life with yourself and your family.

The last one on the list ruled my life. As a "start-up" guy living in the geographically compact Silicon Valley, I was surrounded by entrepreneurs who burned themselves out for one, two or three years and had reaped the huge payout. They occurred to me as living proof that sacrificing your life for the big check was a smart move.

My ego gravitated toward this belief. I had friends who "hit" it big and chose to take a year off to travel the world. One of them sold his company, bought a boat and sailed the world for a year.

The divine had other plans for my life, apparently, and lessons for me to learn that I was to share with the world:

- I lived two miles from Mark Zuckerberg while he was building Facebook with his buddies. Two miles. •

The Google founders were hacking away at Stanford, three miles from my house. My friend, who may have worse luck than I do, met them and received a demonstration of their new search technology—before it was funded. They offered to let him invest $10,000 as an angel investor. He passed. That sum, if invested then, would now be worth tens of millions of dollars, if not more.

- An investor in one of my companies had to leave a meeting with me because some "guys with a taxi service called Uber" were waiting in the lobby. He funded them and rolled off my company's board of directors.

- While sitting at a bar in San Francisco with a friend of mine, I was introduced to a guy who had strung together some code that pushed advertising messages through text around the world and generated real-time feedback. His next stop that afternoon was a venture capital firm. He landed $5 million that day, and within 12 months, Google bought his company for $750 million.

Ideas and success are everywhere in Silicon Valley. Even as pervasive as minted millionaires are, they are still the minority of wealth holders. Real estate owners— people who maintain steady jobs, keep their mortgages current and reap the rewards of sky-high property value increases— hold most of the Valley's wealth.

It is easy to get caught up in the idea that money can be easily created with hard work and that working for money is worth what occurs as a "short term" sacrifice. However,

45

any belief that separates your personal life from your business life creates a false dichotomy.

There is no separation between the two. None. All that exists is your life as framed by the time you have on the planet. The only time you are guaranteed is the present moment. The past doesn't exist. If it did, you could go back to it. The future also doesn't exist. Both are concepts formed by your mind.

THE ONLY TIME YOU ARE GUARANTEED IS THE PRESENT MOMENT.

Think about it. There's just you and the present moment in which you exist. Now, let's extend that concept into the reality of business.

STORIES IN YOUR MIND ABOUT BUSINESS
Archeologists believe our human ancestors spent most of their time foraging for food and sleeping. As our species evolved, we began to make tools to help us harvest or kill food, build shelters and craft utensils for cooking.

For most of human history, up to the Age of Industry, people lived an agrarian life focused on staying alive. Even those early entrepreneurs who ventured to create livings by providing goods or services often still had small farms or gardens and hunted for their protein.

The focus for most of our human history was on sustaining life. Activities were not separated between "work" and "personal life." It was just life and living day- to-day, moment by moment. Families lived together and supported each other in the daily grind to stay alive. The family unit was, in a way, the first business. It was real and tangible. Business was simply the activities people did.

STORY 1: MY BUSINESS IS SEPARATE FROM MYSELF.

In 1602, however, the activities people did to sustain life were assigned for the first time to an abstraction of reality called the East India Company. The Dutch government granted the world's first corporation exclusive rights to all trade with India, personifying the corporation as an entity bigger and with greater longevity than the investors who created it. The East India Company would continue to trade with India long after the people who originally comprised it were dead.

Since then, corporations have gradually embedded themselves into the human psyche as something almost human. Because a corporation is assigned rights and can accept liability for the actions of the people who work for it, our language now makes little distinction between the notion of a business entity that exists only on paper and a human, who exists.

Consider the colloquialisms:
- I work for Company X.
- Company X is corrupt.
- Company X is growing rapidly.
- Company X is dying.

- I hate Company X.
- I love Company X.
- Company X has an outstanding mission.
- Company X has a great vision for future products.
- Company X is moving me to another state.
- My company is taking a lot of my time.
- I need to spend time with the company.

You are also living within this tragic cultural disambiguation. Legally, there is a distinction between the business and you. The former exists for the protection of the latter. However, when this disambiguation is extended into the strategies generated for a living, and we believe that the business is separate from ourselves, then we begin to manage in two different buckets.

_____ STORY 2: I HAVE TWO BUCKETS OF TIME TO MANAGE.

When we believe that time is bifurcated, our mind creates one bucket of time for activities that occur to sustain life and one for everything that does not happen as life supporting. Naturally, it prioritizes the former ahead of the latter.

By categorizing activities that sustain life as related to a personified concept of business only, our tendency will always be to take the currency from the personal bucket and give it to the business bucket.

STORY 3: BUSINESS ALONE IS THE ONLY LIFESUSTAINING ACTIVITY.

We are all born pre-programmed with a survival instinct. We will defend ourselves when threatened and focus our energies on efforts we believe will preserve and extend our body's life on earth. These impulses of the physical form will lead us toward activities that make the body feel good and occur to preserve itself. Instinctive preservation worked well when we were evolving but can create conflict now that we are sentient.

The arrival of intelligence coordinates with religious and spiritual beliefs that believe God created a soul and placed it into a human form that already existed. With the advent of the spirit, we became more than evolved animals that blindly followed our survival instinct. Our spirit also needed to be fed with the same concern we'd exhibit for our bodies. What the spirit needs, however, is much different than the body. Spirit needs love, community and connection. It does not like to be lonely or isolated, and it can become spiritually exhausted.

When we believe that our work is the only lifesustaining activity, then we prioritize our time spend into that bucket and the expense of other activities that sustain our spirit and enhance the quality of our time on earth into another bucket?

Spirit and body need to be in the balance with each other. When we invest too much time in the business, we decrease the time we spend with family, our God, ourselves in

meditation, community to give back and other activities that, although not money generating,
have been scientifically proven to keep our physical bodies healthy and even lengthen life.

When we serve the business at the expense of the spirit, anxiety and depression increase—both of which take a toll on the body and can lead to its ultimate demise.

STORY 4: THE BUSINESS CAN'T LIVE WITHOUT ME.

If you feel the business can't live without you, then it may be controlling you. Most of the people I coach have a dream of "one day" spending more time with the family or taking more vacations. When I ask them what prevents them from doing so now, their consistent replies are:

- The business won't let me.
- My business is just keeping me too busy.
- If I left for two weeks in a row, my business would collapse.
- I'm in growth mode—it's all hands-on deck here.
- I'm losing revenue and shrinking now; I need to focus on getting things back in order.

While those replies may be true contemporaneously with the question being asked, they do not necessarily have to be true in the future. Well-run and managed enterprises, no matter how large or small, can—and should—run without the CEO and owner on premise all the time.

LEADERS AREN'T FOLLOWERS AND ARCHITECTS DON'T BUILD—THEY CONTROL AND DEFINE THE SHAPE AND DESTINY OF WHAT OTHERS ARE TO HELP MAKE.

Control, however, is an illusion. And it is an illusion that starts at home—with the self. If you are truly in control of self, then the business can't control you. In most cases, however, we look outside self at what we occur to control—cash flow, some employee behavior (more influencing and directing than controlling), product development, marketing spend and not much else.

We see ourselves as masters of our fate, leading a symphony of our making. In reality, our egos have shackled ourselves to our business and jobs. We believe we are invaluable and without our contribution, the business could not flourish. These are ego-driven, selflimiting beliefs that I've seen tamp company growth and even lead to a company's demise.

When we choose to believe that others could run the business as well, if not better, than we are, then we are open to testing that assumption by gradually releasing control to others.

When we release control, we become more valuable to those to whom control is released and free our minds to think strategically. That freedom may release new products and services into the market and help increase the stability and long-term viability of your company and your legacy.

We only become as important as we think we are when we choose to view ourselves as expendable.

To illustrate this point, let's revisit the case study of Curt Vander Meer, the CEO of Endangered Species Chocolate we mentioned in the opening chapter.

Curt Vander Meer

As we covered earlier, Curt struggled to understand how fusing life and business into one strategic and intentional plan made any sense and could impact his business. While in a board meeting with his Vistage peer group, he admitted that one thing he wanted most of all was to take an entire month off from the business. He picked the month of July 2019, three years after he began his 12-quarter plan.

After identifying it as the goal, he then realized that the reason he can't take time off now and hasn't been able to do so for 18 years is that he had been managing the company as what he calls a CEO-centric organization that was far too dependent on him. To take the vacation, he needed a different management structure in place before July 2019. He began building two tiers of management with directors to direct and managers to manage. He started efforts to reshape the company culture to one more empowered to make decisions without him and less fearful of failing. He brought in consultants to train the company on the Rockefeller Habits.

His movement and action to create the world in which he could take four weeks off from the business began by ignoring the limiting belief that the business couldn't live without him. This lead to a choice he made to create the world in which he could be absent from the business for four contiguous weeks, which then created a plan and actions that were filtered throughout the entire company. The result of simply bending the business around a personal goal to take more vacation time dramatically reshaped his organization and made it stronger and more valuable.

Curt didn't stop with vacation time. He chose to have Endangered Species Chocolate give $1 million —10 percent of its net profits—away to charities that protect endangered species around the world. To do that by his deadline, he'd have to double profits. A stronger management team free to make more decisions is one way to help get profits up over three years. If profits are up, revenues likely are as well. (I know his plan did not call for cost cutting his way to increased net profit.)

"Before I engaged with this 12-quarter process," Curt said, "I would say 'someday' I'll do this or that. Now, I am dissecting everything that needs to happen for my 'someday' to be realized and then executing on those things within 12 quarters.

I believe the real power behind this process is that it allows one to run a company with intention. The message of having the business work for me and not the other way around actually spoke to me. It made me realize that while I valued time with family higher than time on the business, my life wasn't reflecting that as consistently as I would have liked. I don't want that time to slip away, and now I'm operating in a way that it won't."

One of the reasons we get into the trap of working for the business or feeling like slaves to it is because our minds tend to personify our company as if it were a sentient entity that needs to be served.

STORY 5: BUSINESS IS "SOMEONE"

Business, however, is not sentient. It is a concept that exists only in legal documents and not in reality. You cannot find or interact with Apple, Google or any other entity that is incorporated because they don't exist.

That said, what is business or work or career? They are nothing more than words for categories of activities we do to earn a living and sustain part, not all, of our needs.

Business doesn't exist. Business-related activities, however, do exist in reality.

- The business, while legally distinct, is not different from you. You conduct activities, some of which are related to business.
- There is only one bucket of time, not two: the time you are given.
- Your body and spirit are equally important; focusing on the survival of the body through business activities alone can lead to depression, anxiety, regret, guilt and other negative and debilitating emotions.
- Others in the world can conduct your business activities as well, if not better, than you can.

To help model these changes in perspective for the rest of this book, I am going to shift from using the term *business* to something more accurate: *business activities.*

This subtle shift in language changes the way business occurs as a personified "something or someone" we serve to the reality of what it is: activities we do to earn a living. It accomplishes this shift in the following steps:

1. Without personification, it is harder to assign responsibility for your choices to something that doesn't exist. The business can't be blamed for taking too much time, for instance.

2. By not blaming others—even a personified non-entity—we accept responsibility for our choices.

3. By taking responsibility, we gain control.

4. When we gain control, what we are controlling is our time.

5. When we realize we are controlling time, we are controlling the activities we choose to do during the time we have.

6. From this new perch of personal control over our operations and responsibility for directing them, we can begin to balance our lifesustaining activities around things we want to do, not just business activities.

7. When we start to balance our time between categories of life-sustaining activities, we can then start to bend the business activities to support the goals and objectives we currently hold in high esteem and are impossible to achieve.

8. When the business activities are bent around what we want to do—those passions—we can build a plan that creates the desired outcome in 12 quarters.

9. That which was once considered impossible becomes possible; that which was found to be unattainable is attained.

TRANSFORMATION 2: BELIEVE THAT ALL SITUATIONS AND EVENTS ARE NEUTRAL Vedanta is an ancient spiritual philosophy based on the Vedas (knowledge) of the sacred scriptures of India. The goals of the tradition are to help people have direct experience with their real nature. One of the concepts covered in their practice is the idea that there are four steps our minds follow to understanding and deciphering the world around us. My friend and fellow business coach, Jay Steven Levin, likes to call these steps our "slippery slide to delusion," a somewhat tongue-incheek description of the conclusions our mind reaches at times.

These four steps are followed for any event you witness— including a light bulb being turned on, a car backing out of the drive, a strange sound echoing in your home, you name it. All events go through the same fourstep sequence. They are:

1. Observe—your mind sees the event.
2. Classify—your mind classifies the event into a category of good, bad, neutral, interesting, boring, right or wrong.
3. Personalize—your mind then takes the event and makes it relevant to you.
4. Emotionalize—anger, frustration, joy, happiness, and emotion happen at this step.

These four steps help us understand how and when we emotionalize events and how emotions affect our behavior. The intent, when becoming mindful of this processing technique our brains use, is to allow emotions to pass through us rather than controlling our actions. We can then intentionally move "back up" to the observation point to clearly see what occurred.

WHAT HAPPENS WHEN WE OBSERVE AN EVENT

Observing an event is called the neutral position because the mind has not yet taken the remaining three steps in the event-framing process. Remember, events are neutral until you place meaning and judgment on them.

Let's look at this idea of neutrality using an extreme example of someone witnessing a possible murder.

Example
Citizen Bob is standing on a street corner waiting for his Uber® driver when he hears a gunshot nearby. He looks down the alley and sees a person grab their stomach, slouch to the ground and then appear to die. He did not see the

shooter and did not witness the gun being fired. Following the four ways we frame events, here is one likely scenario Bob's brain may create.

1. Observe: Person is shot, this is what I observe.
2. Classify: This was murder.
3. Personalize: This event affects me.
4. Emotionalize: I'm scared for my safety.

The event that happened, however, is that someone was shot. There's no evidence that the person is dead or that the event is murder. Bob's classifying, personalizing and emotionalizing of the event will lead to an action he will take.

Bob's brain, just like your mind, went through these four steps in less than a second. The action Bob takes is to run to the nearest coffee shop before calling the police. To choose the coffee shop, his brain went through all four steps again: the shop was observed, classified as safe, personalized as "Bob's safe place" and emotionalized as a spot that will relieve Bob's anxiety.
Bob is now in the coffee shop and dials 911.

The gunshot victim is not dead, however. He lies in the alley bleeding and holding his midsection. The dispatcher receives Bob's call and immediately relays it to the officer closest to the scene of the incident. Upon arrival, the trained officer views the scene and processes it much differently than Bob did.

1. Observe: The dispatcher called me and said a man named Bob witnessed a shooting and is now sitting in a coffee shop.

58

2. Personalize: Because I am on duty, this is my event to investigate.
3. Classify: I won't categorize the event until I see the evidence. Based on the evidence I discover, I will then classify the event as murder (wrong), suicide (bad choice) or justifiable homicide.

Noticeably absent from the law enforcement's process is personal "emotionalizing" of the event. Classification is reserved until enough information is gathered to judge and categorize the event correctly.

The officer discovers that the victim is not dead, but rather critically wounded—and much closer to dying than they would have been had Bob immediately tended to the wound and called 911.

The officer calls for an ambulance.

A shooting most always occurs as an adverse situation. In reality, the only judgment that can be immediately placed on the shooting is that the presence of a bullet in someone's body is detrimental to good health. That's not even a judgment; it is a fact.

After tending to the wound and calling for the ambulance, the officer checks the victim's identification and discovers that he is a serial killer wanted as a suspect in a recent murder. A shaken woman with a gun in her hand walks up to the officer and confesses to shooting the man in self-defense.

What are you observing as this story unfolds? The facts are changing the way the situation is classified, right? The event itself was neutral. A person was shot.

To the criminal, a bullet in his body occurs as an adverse situation. To the shooter who was acting in self-defense, the police who could apprehend a violent perpetrator, and the local community, the event of that criminal being shot may occur as good. The actual event—what happened—is simply an event.

The case of someone being shot is extreme and was chosen for that reason. When we open our minds to the fact that even a violent situation is just an event when first observed, then we can shift more fluidly to the belief that all events are neutral.

You, me and everyone else on the planet determine how to classify situations. And we classify situations based on how they occur. Situations occur to us differently, depending, in part, on the self-limiting beliefs and interjections each of us has in our minds.

Some of the self-limiting beliefs that helped frame the way the situation occurred to Bob are:

1. I shouldn't help the victim because I'm not trained.
2. I should call the police only once I am safe.
3. I should run to a coffee shop because it is safe.
4. I could be sued by the victim if I try to aid and fail.

5. I should assume the shooter is dangerous.
6. When I was a child, my mother told me I was weak and couldn't stand up for myself against bullies so I should just run and hide.

The list can continue. As the sixth point illustrates, limiting beliefs can have their origin in childhood. To be clear, Bob's decisions, being based on his life experiences, were not "wrong." It's simply the way Bob reacted.

Primum non nocere—First, do no harm.

I have coached the right/wrong concept to enough people to realize that some will interpret the concept of event neutrality as the antithesis to their moral beliefs and deeply held religious convictions. Morality is simply a list of actions with events classified based on the likely intent of the individual who did the deed. *Intent* and *motive* go together.

For example, a person cuts another person. If the injury was intended to cause violent murder, we might judge that as "bad." If the wound was caused by a surgeon attempting to relieve suffering, we might classify it as a "good" or "right" action.

The Hippocratic Oath states, "First, do no harm." Events, generally speaking, are judged by the intent to harm or not harm others.

TRANSFORMATION 3: BELIEVE THAT CLASSIFICATIONS OF RIGHT/WRONG AND SUCCESS/FAILURE ARE SELF-LIMITING

Some of the most commonly debilitating auto-reflexive classifications used are "right/wrong," "success/failure" and "good/bad." The context within which we'll be working for the rest of this book is outside theological and moral event classifications.

To get your mind moving in the right direction, choose one of the following:

1. I prefer to hire a person who will get the job I need done, done.
2. I prefer to hire a person who will get the job I need done, done right.

This question is called a bias question, and I use it frequently to help people see their biases. In most every case, people look at me sideways. Maybe you're doing that too, right now.

Good. Hold on that curiosity. I'll address it later.

FAILURE

Let's first look at failure. Failure is a judgment word that Webster's dictionary defines as "lack of success." Unfortunately, the word is quite often used and personalized as a *character* trait applied to people, things and events. "I am a *failure,*" *or* "She is a *failure*" are all too common misuses of the word. When *failure* is personalized in such a way, it is charged with negative emotion. The same is true for failure's counterpart, *success.* It, too, is often personalized and applied, as adjectives to ourselves or others. In reality, both *failure* and *success* should not be personalized and applied to people. They are too imprecise. The ambiguity and emotional energy of both words make them poor choices to use in daily conversation.

In both life *and* business management, it is best to do away with the words *failure* and *success* because they are so emotionally charged, judgment based and, in many cases, applied to events or people by our inherent biases and not the reality of the facts we observe.

One person's success may also be another person's failure. To avoid the emotional impact of those two words in your life and leadership, we need to change the language to something more aligned with what happened. Lack of achievement, rather than failure, is a less charged description, as is its opposite: achievement.

When we set a goal and do not meet the goal, we didn't fail. We simply did not achieve or attain the target. Conversely, when we succeed, all we did was achieve/attain that which we sought to reach or complete. With achievement, the result of the actions will exist in the physical world. With the lack of progress or partial achievement, there is also manifestation in the real world because what it was we sought to do or create did not end up existing.

Failure is a judgment. Two people can look at the same achievement and judge it differently.

Coffee machines may stop working. That's the event. The coffee maker stopped working. When it stopped working, it did not make coffee. We may attach the concept of failure to the event that the coffee maker stopped working: "The coffee maker failed to make coffee." But to someone who does not like coffee, that same event may occur as a success: "The smell of coffee makes me sick, and this morning the coffee machine broke, and I successfully made it out the door without becoming nauseous."

The point in all of this is to begin to open our minds to the reality that all events are neutral, judgments are entirely subjective and meanings like *success* and *failure* are only attached to events by our inherent biases.

We can choose to reframe the personalization and emotionalization of how we see and experience events. During your 12-quarter journey, you will be tempted to judge yourself based on the results your actions generated. That judgment can impair decision making. Understanding that all events are neutral is critical to being able to see clearly what *is*.

GOOD OR BAD

Events are neither good nor bad. They are neutral until a framework—meaning—is applied to them and a judgment attached. That framework can be provided by religion, politics, social upbringing and your life experiences.

The good/bad judgments are particularly nefarious and insidious in business. While success and failure can be logically attached to events by our biases—and more easily unattached from them—good/bad language is charged with emotions generated in part by moral biases. Think about it: good children get presents; bad children don't. Our societal biases toward those words frame them in a moral context with applied meaning that typically leads to a rather binary decision process: we will do what is good and not do what is bad (at least those are the objectives).

Because our minds are programmed to react to those two words with only a binary set of solutions, events deemed as "bad," for instance, may quickly and irrationally be course-corrected toward things considered as good, whereas events deemed "good" may be doubled down on without thinking them through.

One event that consistently traps small to medium size companies is landing the business of a much larger company. Initially, the event is judged as "good" for the company as it provides stable revenue. However, large companies often sap the resources of small ones, trapping them in a viscous vacuum that creates a significant single point of failure for the small business.

I've coached business owners who relied on one company for 40 percent or more of their revenue. I judged that situation as "dangerous" rather than "good" for the life of their company, as it created a single point of failure that could decimate their business should the large account be cancelled.

The owner agreed in principle to the concept and began working to re-balance the portfolio. The urgency to rebalance wasn't there because the revenue was so consistent. And then it happened. The larger company was bought, and the acquiring company canceled the business of the smaller one. In just four weeks, the small company went from fat and happy to starving and on the verge of going under.

Is landing a large, fat and consistently paying account "good" or "bad"? It's neither; it just is. What matters most is how the company and the revenue from the account are managed. Had my small client immediately and urgently begun to diversify their sources of income, the large account would have been viewed as a funding mechanism for growth.

What made the difference in managing that account? The way it was judged. Judgment is powerful and subjective; it drives our actions and creates results. Judging a primary account as *good* leads to a binary decision path that simply maintained the status quo
rather than actively working to adjust it for the health of the company.

RIGHT OR WRONG

Right / Wrong judgments are incredibly charged with meaning and often can be void of any compassion. There is a "right" way to do something and a "wrong" way to do the same thing, we often are told. These two words hardly leave open space for alternative viewpoints and methodologies.

In my experience, business owners who adopt "right and wrong" language are more likely to rebuff attempts to innovate their processes, improve their companies or enhance their product or service. They are also less likely to reframe their worldview as judging something as "right" has moral associations, as does judging the event as "wrong."

Remember the bias question asked at the beginning of this chapter?

"Do you prefer to hire someone who will just do the job you have or do it right?"

- If you prefer to get it done "right" then you have a preconceived bias toward what "right" is in your context that is likely based on many factors, the most prominent of which is that you've created processes and procedures that you determine to be the right way to do things in your business. You very likely will not be open to a candidate who will bring in his or her processes and procedures.

- If you prefer just to get the job done, then you're signaling an openness to candidates who may have their own teams, processes or procedures and will bring them to work for you—at the expense of the ones you've already created.

There is no "right" way to answer this question. Franchises like McDonald's don't hire people who will get things done; they hire only those who will get it done "right," as defined by their time-tested protocols for successfully winning in the fast food industry.

EMOTIONS & ENERGY CREATED BY JUDGMENT

Humans aren't robots, and while technically we can choose how to feel about things emotionally, judgment words do generate emotions when they are heard and absorbed by our mind. Emotions are energy. Positive emotions produce activity and creativity; negative emotions drain us of both and leave us tired, weary and fearful.

When we judge an event as a failure, we may feel dejected, resigned and less motivated to find success. When we judge an event as successful, we may have much more positive energy and feel more vibrant and confident.

By not judging events immediately until all the data are properly reviewed, we are better able to remain in a steady state of emotion. Neutrality of judgment allows a safe, peaceful space to form in our minds and our emotional core.

Consider the following example statements:

1. We succeeded in meeting our quarterly revenue objectives!
2. We made $X in revenue, and that revenue achieved the goal we established for the quarter.
3. We failed to meet our quarterly objectives.
4. We achieved revenues of $X this quarter and that number was $X shy of the goal we established.

In the first example, the word "success" will attach to two events simultaneously: a) the revenue generated and b) the goal itself. Both occur as successful. The actions likely to be taken from reading this sentence are to continue whatever actions led to the goal being met.
Why upset the proverbial apple cart?

In the second example, hitting the revenue target is stated objectively. There is no sense that a) the company would celebrate hitting the target or, more importantly, that b) the company views the goal as something worth hitting in the first place. The actions that could come from this sentence are a) continued review of the goal— is it correctly calibrated to the actual market opportunity?—and b) how did we hit that goal—was it one large customer that we won't have next quarter?

By removing judgment, we open the door for honest, pragmatic exploration of events. By adding judgment, we risk closing doors and our minds to alternative realities that exist and should be known.

In example three, we feel the dejection of failure as it is juxtaposed with its neutral counterpoint in example four. Failure is a powerful emotion that can lead to anxiety, inaction or overreaction that isn't necessary.

The company did not make the quarterly goal. That is the event. Why didn't it make the goal? Did the sales team extend its absolute best efforts and the executive team simply over-estimated market demand? When the word *failure* is attached, things become personal.

In one of the companies I founded with five other friends of mine, we had seven consecutive quarters with 40 percent (+) quarter-on-quarter growth rates. And then a major competitor dropped a product into our marketplace and told its sales team to give the product away, if necessary, to beat my company. The opponent calculated that it would be cheaper to put us out of business by dumping its product into our market than buying my company. The opponent was right. And on the eight-quarter, our revenues plummeted. Our sales team "failed" to meet the quarterly goals we established.
They were dejected.

They "failed" again in quarter nine. And ten. And eleven. This "failure" came despite the efforts we undertook to establish reasonable goals that were in line with new market conditions.

Was the sales team failing? Was my company failing? It felt like it. The answer, however, is "no." When we started to look at the events as neutral, they occurred this way:

1. We have a great product people want to buy and competitors are afraid our product's ability to achieve market share will damage their hold on this segment.
2. We don't have the cash to win against a publicly traded company willing to give its product away.
3. To continue as a viable business, we need to pivot into a space free of this competitor.

71

When we stopped thinking we were failing and started to view events as neutral, we stopped trying to succeed in a market where we could no longer compete. You could argue that we were achieving all that we could achieve given the rapidly changing market conditions. Our plan was unrealistic, sure. But the sales team was gathering all the revenue it could. So, what was failing?

We weren't *failures*. We just needed to move into a different market to achieve the revenue numbers necessary to keep investors happy and people employed. And we did. The actions we took were aggressive: we cut marketing, invested more in engineering, dropped our sales targets to be congruent with the new market conditions until we were ready to move into another market and built a new product that has since won
numerous awards and had no competitor for about 12 months. Here's another way to look at it. If your company is only capable of collecting 100 blue marbles in a sea of a million red, green and orange marbles—and it collects them—did it fail because it didn't collect other colored marbles? Of course not. Market conditions changed suddenly for my company, putting the other colors out of our reach.

As a business owner, it is imperative to be able to assess events without bias and with curiosity as they come speeding toward you. Jumping to conclusions with judgment-based language can severely limit the options your mind generates.

If we attach judgment words to events, the emotional highs or lows associated with analysis can accelerate us in the wrong direction or stymie us from doing anything at all.

STORIES CREATED BY JUDGMENT

Judgment builds stories and belief systems that create strongholds in our minds. A stronghold is a fortified building—think of a castle. The idea here is that the belief is very hard to breach with new ideas and even harder to destroy and replace with new ideas.

When an event is declared "right" or "wrong," for instance, our minds may program themselves to believe that similar events are either "right" or "wrong." I've run into this stronghold time and time again in my coaching and consulting work. The typical story is that a strategy or idea didn't work once in a previous company or job and was judged as "failed." It doesn't even matter
if the last attempt was with a different product, market and price point. If the strategy didn't work once, it failed, and failed strategies are wrong ways of doing business. Once an approach is deemed wrong and a failure, it is now a belief applied continually to all businesses and products and markets. Strategies aren't the only subjects that fall prey to eternal judgment. I've hired employees who rejected my open-door, inclusive management style because their previous work experiences taught them that "all managers are reclusive and non-caring."

Events are neutral. When a strategy does not drive anticipated results, it doesn't mean the strategy has "failed." It doesn't mean anything, just like one reclusive boss does not represent or define all employers. When we look at events and situations as neutral, our minds can remain open to new possibilities and not closed by false beliefs whose only relation to reality is in our minds.

In your 12-quarter plan, you will run into events and situations that will test your ability to remain neutral. Think about those strategies or ideas that may not have worked in other cases and could work now. Keep your mind open as you build the plan and don't assume anything is true based on past experiences.

"WE NEED TO ACCEPT THAT WE WON'T ALWAYS MAKE THE RIGHT DECISIONS, THAT WE'LL SCREW UP ROYALLY SOMETIMES— UNDERSTANDING THAT FAILURE IS NOT THE OPPOSITE OF SUCCESS, IT IS PART OF SUCCESS." ARIANNA HUFFINGTON

VIEW OF SELF CREATED BY JUDGMENT

The most extensive damage created by judgment is the view of self. When we attach judgment to an event and then responsibility for that event upon ourselves, the subjective classification of that event is often attached to our identity.

Our ego-mind has a penchant for making itself the center of the universe and the first cause of all things. The ego wants to take credit for everything and loves to wallow in its pool of self-pity. It loves excuses to protect itself from further pain and knows no bounds. Its only focus is on itself, often to our detriment.

The ego-mind is you, but if you're mindful of how it operates, then you can choose to think differently. I realize we're getting a little metaphysical. Consider it this way: whoever or whatever you are (your essence) can be mindful of itself and the tricks its ego component will play. Ego is not pride or arrogance; it is the part of self that works only to preserve self and draw attention to self.

When an event occurs that did not meet our expectations for it or the expectation of others, we can take that "failure" personally. Most egos personalize the failure, making themselves "the failure" and even drawing attention of others to the lack of success in a paradoxical attempt to claim authority and power for all that happens, both good and bad, because the reward most egos seek is attention. That said, this is not a book about enlightenment, so I'm going to go no deeper than these few paragraphs. If you'd like to learn more about this concept, yourself and those who work for you, read Eckhart Tolle's *The Power of Now*.

Here are a few examples of how we personalize failure:

- "I" failed to hit the sales goal.
- "I" failed; therefore, I must be a failure.
- "I" am a failure at sales and I don't want to look bad or hurt anymore because of it.
- "I" will not try selling anything again.

When we view ourselves as failures, we are damaging the very nature that can provide the energy needed to continue or redirect our paths. Success can also become part of an individual's identity—to their detriment.

- "I" built a great product people bought.
- "I" hired 100 people.
- "I" sold my company for a lot of money.
- "I" am successful.
- "I" will do the same thing I did before when I build my new company.

We've all likely met people who have this last script programmed into their egos. They are unmanageable for a time and can't be taught anything new. Silicon Valley is ripe with these egos. A young person gets funded and instantly becomes a "CEO"—with zero previous leadership experience. The success they attribute to raising money attaches to their identity, and they believe they are a successful CEO. This is the insanity of the ego-mind as created and fueled by judgment words.

In one of the companies I worked with, it became apparent that the only way the CEO would mature was by letting him experience events that did not and could not be judged as successful. The investor, deeming their bet on the company no longer optimal because the CEO was demonstrating a "tin ear," as they called it, stopped funding the company. The CEO's plans could not be realized without cash or a team, and he soon learned the hard lesson that just because some events went per a plan he had in mind once in his life, that did not mean he was a god who could create and shape events per his will.

Egos cloud judgment. They frame events based on biases, personalize both success and failure and shape the truth of what happened into something different. The result: a cloudy view of reality that can negatively impact our ability to make the best decisions.

APPLICATION TO YOUR 12-QUARTER PLAN

You're likely wondering how all this applies to your 12quarter plan.

The first step in the 12-quarter plan is to create an Outcome Statement. And what you begin to write will likely occur to you as impossible to achieve. Your mind will race through every limiting belief that has prevented you from seeing your desired outcome as achievable.

Then, it will disregard certain things as not worth writing down or thinking about, and finally, it will reach into the past as an indicator of what is possible in the future. In business, we call this last point "forecasting based on actuals."

If you write an Outcome Statement based on your past personal, professional or business performance, you're not going to change a thing. To change, you need to transform the way the future can look and your way of viewing the future.

If you've always wanted to take five weeks off from the business and it's never occurred as possible, then take the first step to changing the way that situation occurs and place it in your Outcome Statement.

If you have preconceived biases toward what "right" is, realize that those biases can simultaneously serve as limiting beliefs. Be open to exploring other ideas your mind may bring to you during this process. Realize that "right" is subjective and you have the power to choose how to redefine it at any time.

Here are a few exercises to help continue the transformation process.

Exercise 1:

1. Think of a situation in your business. It could be anything—revenues are soaring/falling, margins are fat/skinny, employees are pleasant/pains in the backside…. you get the idea. Describe each situation on a separate sheet of paper. For instance, you could write, "I have a lazy employee who does nothing but cause trouble."

2. Review the description you just wrote. Now describe how that situation is occurring in your mind and emotionally. For instance, "The lazy employee problem occurs as a situation that is harming morale and becoming unmanageable. I don't have time for their crap, and it's driving me crazy, consuming far more time than I want and is something I must address soon before it does permanent damage to my business."

3. Now write down three possible actions you could take to resolve the issue you've described and the timeframe in which you could take those actions.

TRANSFORMATION 4: BELIEVE THAT ALTERNATIVE PLANS TO YOUR GOALS WILL BE REVEALED—AND THAT'S OKAY.

In most cultures, life is presented as a timeline that has a beginning and an end. What happens in between is anyone's guess and is usually out of our control for the most part, yet we spend an ocean's worth of energy trying to direct events before and while they unfold.

In business, this exercise manifests as a strategic plan and financial plan. Each year, good business owners sit down and plot a revenue course for their companies and a plan to achieve that revenue. The events we anticipate will happen (revenue or margin growth, new products being launched, etc.) are called assumptions for a reason: we don't know if those events will occur, but we use data, research, intuition and third-party advice as foundations to help make the assumptions more congruent with a reality that could happen.

Despite the frequent use of terms like *forecast* and *assumption*, we treat our plans as if they are prophecy. Forecasts based on even the best assumptions are still far from prophetic.

To make things even worse on our psyche, we graphically represent our assumption-based forecast
linearly, like the example to the right. This linear representation is a financial metaphor that our mind relates directly to its real-world, physically manifested counterpart: the path or road.

A road is an established and widely available tool for getting from point A to point B quickly and accurately with little confusion. A
road does start
somewhere and end
somewhere else
predictably. If we're
paying attention to
which road we choose
(admittedly, I've ended
up on freeways to somewhere, but nowhere near my target destination) we know the road will take us to our destination. No one ever says I'm forecasting that the 405 will take me from Long Beach to the 10. We know that the 405 takes me there.

The figure below illustrates the judgment language associated with the linear progression model. If we achieve our goal "G," you may view that situation as "success" and have the corresponding emotional uplift.
If what you produce falls "short" of the goal, the words "failure to meet the goal" is usually attached to that situation. If events not only take us off plan but backward (revenue losses, etc.), that reversal can occur as a setback.

When you're looking at that chart, what emotions arise around the word *setback*? *Failure* and *success*? Emotions are energy. What type of energy surrounds those words? Is it Positive? Negative? Apathetic?

Linear expectations invoke stress when markets don't cooperate.

	Sometimes, we go backward.	Our achievement falls short.	Goal is set and a plan built.
	Reversal	**A**chieved	**G**oal
How events are perceived	**S**etback	**F**ailure	**S**uccess

THE SNIPE HUNT FOR THE SELF-FULFILLING PROPHECY

We treat our models, forecasts and assumptions as divine revelations. Wall Street holds CEOs accountable to achieving their forecasts and punishes them by selling off stock if they don't. CEOs, in turn, drive their executive teams to stay "on plan" and those teams, in turn, motivate their employees on the same quest.

What Western culture has created is nothing more than a snipe hunt to find a self-fulfilling prophecy. CEOs are not prophets, and the models they build are not scripture; they're just guesses.

In reality, life does not actualize predictably in a straight line from point A to point B and, for the most part, we can't

81

create long-term or "forward-looking" prophecies that we can then fulfill to the degree of accuracy we— and others— expect ourselves to achieve.

NOT FINDING THE SNIPE CANCELS THE HUNT

Everything that happens is an event, and as we covered previously, all events are neutral. When our predictions do not come true, we typically will judge the event through the lens of our biases and use judgment words to describe the event. How many times have you heard the phrase "failed to meet expectations"? More than you can count, probably.

When judgment-based language is used to describe events as they occur through the lens of predictions generated with assumptions that are modeled and graphically represented in a linear progression, conclusions are drawn that may be disconnected from what happened—the actual event.

Example: Event: Fourth quarter sales goals were $10 million; actual sales were $9 million during that period. The business language used to describe the event: "Fourth quarter sales failed to meet plan." As we discussed in a previous chapter, the business language will drive the quest to find out what went wrong and who is responsible. CEOs and their employees are constantly under stress to prove themselves prophets of their destiny.

THERE IS NO SNIPE. OUR FORECASTS DON'T EXIST.

Life, however, is not predictable, and it's better to choose not to view events as linear progressions of the situations that occurred before them. Events are just events; they are not bound to build upon each other to create the model we have in our minds. Dating does not always lead to engagement and marriage. Marriage does not always result in a suburban cottage, a dog and then children. Saving money does not guarantee savings will grow and money will be saved. Working out and eating healthy does not mean your body will remain healthy.

You get the idea. While saving money is wise to do, expecting that the value of our savings will grow linearly unabated is not aligned with reality. Healthy lifestyles are also wise to maintain, but assuming that a healthy lifestyle will ensure that you remain healthy will only lead to disillusionment if events take your health in an unhealthy direction.

Buddhism teaches this principle within the framework of non-attachment. All our anxieties, fears and stresses have a single source: emotional and spiritual attachment to people, things and expectations we do not and cannot control. When we choose to observe events rather than manipulate or control them, we can come closer to a state of peace, at least in relation to our plans. Our egos will no longer have power over us and keep us chained to the false belief that we can control our destinies to the extent we want to believe.

Our forecasts are guesses at best. Attaching ourselves and others to them emotionally—and physically— generates anxieties that only lead to the lack of clarity and tamp true discovery that may reveal new truths about our plans, markets, behaviors, family, goals and anything else.

With this type of mindfulness will grow a focus on what is paramount—your destination. If events in quarter one do not unfold as you planned, you'll be detached from them enough to devise alternate routes to your desired goals and outcomes.

Back to the example of driving on the 405. If a section of it is under construction, you're not going to insist on taking the 405, right? You—and your GPS—will create alternate routes that still get you to your destination. Did your plan to take the 405 fail? Did you fail because it was under construction? No, of course not. If you arrive at your desired destination, the accuracy of your original plan won't matter.

LIFE UNFOLDS LIKE ITS SOURCE CODE LOOKS— A DIFFERENT WAY OF VIEWING FORECASTS AND PLANS

Life's source code is DNA. It includes all the information to create all life on earth. From mosquitoes to humans, DNA is code that defines how living entities look and operate.

DNA occurs as a double helix, full of twists and turns with connecting rods in between. DNA is not a straight line or a linear progression of code. It's a threedimensional, multi-stranded, information-packed protein that somehow dictates the formation of living organisms. Events, if modeled graphically on a timeline, would look much more like a double helix than they would a linear progression model. If we use the double helix as a mental image of how our plans and forecasts will actualize, we can then take the next step and remove judgment language from our description of events. With a new vocabulary, our energy is not sapped by anxiety and can be spent on new efforts of discovery that are required for our plans to become real.

That's a deep paragraph. Let's build out the concept with a real-world example referencing the figure below.

The image above represents how DNA occurs as a protein. Consider the top strand to be the 12-quarter plan you've built. On it are your ideas for personal, professional and business activities. It's your plan for your life. If you were going to model your plan using the traditional linear model, you'd only see one line: the one you created.

Here, using the double helix, you can see two lines: the one you created and the one that has yet to manifest through events. Already, your mind is prepared—and programmed—to accept unexpected events to occur that may alter your chosen plans. When your mind grasps this concept, it begins to detach emotionally from your plan and becomes open to the truth that **your real job in life is to expect change, not be surprised by it** and not to judge yourself when change comes your way.

Diana Stewart, CEO of Envirox

Envirox produces environmentally safe industrial cleaning products. Several years ago, the company was a category leader with little competition. Times have changed as others locked onto their patents and technologies that began to threaten Diana's company's grip on the market.

One of the most helpful aspects of the 12-quarter planning process, she says, is the concept of the double helix.

"I used to get so emotionally attached to our forecasts and plans," she said. "By detaching from the plan emotionally and believing it is something that *must* work, helps me understand that being off plan is simply "what happened." When I view it more objectively, I can question not just the company's performance, but also the forecast itself," she said. "I ask myself, is the company doing exactly what it is capable of doing and the plan was just off or is the company underperforming? I've since changed my conversations at the executive level from 'how do we get back to plan' to 'is our plan where we still need to be. This is a huge transformation."

For example, her company was planning a big product launch in 2016, and it did not happen on time. In fact, the delay created a large gap in their revenue target for the year. Initially, she wanted to think of this event as a "massive failure" and get stuck in the limiting belief that not reaching their goals would significantly impact the company.

The double helix metaphor helped her remove the emotion from the event and then logically approach the problem from the angle of "What happened?" and not "How do we get back to plan?"

"The helix allowed me to view events as truly neutral and that my job as a CEO was not just about driving a company to plan, but also remaining detached and ready to manage the company as events unfolded."
Changing the way being off plan occurred allowed her to take the constraints off her thinking and see that she should choose a different way to solve what she viewed as a setback. The product would launch; just at another date.

From this new perch of detachment from both her plans and the events that unfold, her mind can think much more creatively.

CHANGE YOUR LANGUAGE

Our word is our thoughts, emotions and intent filtered through language. Word is the "who" you are and the actual purpose and meaning of what is communicated imperfectly through the language codes humans have created.

THE TWO LANGUAGES YOU USE TO COMMUNICATE

Language is a code we use to translate our thoughts and emotions into a physical format that can be reinterpreted by others, thus allowing bilateral, unilateral and multilateral communication to manifest. Our body uses two types of language simultaneously to communicate with others:

- Sounds that form vocabulary that is then reinterpreted by the listener into various meanings based on many factors (environment, upbringing, depth of vocabulary, work and social experiences, etc.). This first form is used to communicate ideas and is not universally translatable from human to human or culture to culture. We typically refer to this as "language."

- Muscle movements in the body, including those that increase the volume, speed and tone by which our tongue and vocal chords form the sound of vocabulary. This second language is universal and often called "body language."

For this chapter, we're going to consider the use of the Word language applying to both the spoken sounds and our body language.

First, let's look at how spoken language alone has a dramatic impact on our everyday life, including how we relate to something as ordinary and universal as mathematics.

Mathematical principles are discovered, not made or created by humans. They're universal within our known universe. Language, therefore, is used to describe mathematical laws and to help our brain use these unbending protocols to solve fundamental problems. If the language we use is inefficient, our speed at problem solving will be reduced.

As Malcolm Gladwell discusses in his book, *The Tipping Point*[2], the Chinese language describes numbers much more efficiently than the English language. This language nuance gives Chinese students an advantage when calculating numbers. This benefit only continues to build upon itself as students learn more complex principles.

Language is responsible for the way numbers occur, not the numbers themselves or the principles behind them. And, the way they occur in our languages directly correlates with the way our students perform in math.

---

[2] Malcolm Gladwell. *The Tipping Point.*

COMMUNICATING YOUR WORD THROUGH LANGUAGE

As we covered in the first chapter, all events are neutral. It's the lens of meaning that we apply to the event that allows us to move through the steps to categorize/judge, personalize and emotionalize the event. Those latter three steps occur in language.

- To classify and personalize the event requires your mind to choose vocabulary, such as good or bad, right or wrong, left or right, etc.
- To communicate our emotionalizing of the event, our brains can instruct our muscles to go rigid, our voice box to increase volume and change tone or any number of other physical reactions and auditory responses.

The observer processes all the data so quickly; we can't easily decipher between the vocabulary we hear and the body language observed. Rather, the mind can often form an immediate conclusion different than the intention of the one communicating. In other words, to the observing mind, language is absorbed and translated simultaneously as one major idea or concept. We do not parse body language from spoken language on the fly, in real time. We simply absorb, classify, personalize and emotionalize based on the entirety of what was communicated.

THE SECOND LAW OF PERFORMANCE: HOW A SITUATION OCCURS ARISES IN LANGUAGE.[3]

---

[3] Steve Zaffron and David Logan, *The Three Laws of Performance*:

Per Zaffron and Logan, situations first occur to us in language. As we go through this concept, keep in mind what you learned about how your brain processes what it hears and fills in the gaps with what it believes to be true.

If all situations occur in language (verbal and body) and 50 percent of that language is an imperfect communication tool that is not universal to the human experience, then there is a good chance that half of what we are communicating or observing isn't completely accurate and the way the situation occurs to us may not be grounded in reality.

To experience this second law, use the examples you wrote down in exercise 1 and run them through exercise 2, below.

Exercise 2:

Let's now focus the lens at you. Think of a situation where the performance of an employee or family member was so unexpected that you felt misunderstood.
You communicated "X," and they did "Y."

1.   What was it you said?
1.   How did you say it?
2.   Were you clear and direct?
3.   What action was the result?
4.   How did that action differ from your expectation of what would happen?

Rewriting the Future of Your Organization and Your Life. (San Francisco: Josse Bass, 2009), 36.

5. How did you feel when the result didn't match the expectation?

6. How did you react when the result didn't match the expectation?

7. Now, give this question your best assumption: If I were to conduct a blind survey of your employees, which behavioral characteristic would they most likely choose to describe how you occur if they could only choose one:

   - Cautious
   - Stable
   - Decisive
   - Friendly

8. With your choice in mind, view your answers from questions 1 and 2 as if you were a thirdparty observer to the situation we're evaluating here. Describe how your employee could have interpreted your words and body language as an intention other than what you felt was being communicated.

For example: "Hey, Frank—can you get me that sales report on last quarter results and oh, wanna grab a beer later?" So, if your employee perceives you as "friendly," it may contribute to the request for the report occurring as not important enough to remember or urgent enough to act upon immediately.

Exercise 3:

1. Now, go back to Exercise 1 and remove all classifying/judging language from your answer. For instance, "I have a lazy employee who does nothing but causes trouble" becomes: "I have an employee who causes trouble."

2. Now review the new, judgment-free statement you just made and re-screen it for classifications that are not blatantly obvious that they're classifications or judgments and replace them with concrete facts. For instance, "I have an employee who causes trouble" now becomes "I have an employee who does not follow the sales process, which diminishes my visibility into sales and makes managing the company more arduous than I believe it should be."

3. How did the way the situation occurs to you change when the language changed?

4. What actions would you take based on the way the situation happened and what actions might you take now that judgment language has been removed?

5. Using the example of the "lazy employee who does nothing but cause problems," we could create mere more actions and results that could have been taken because the employee simply occurred as lazy.

Early on in my career, I was a vice president of a start-up at the young age of 29. Not nuanced in any of the concepts in this book, I routinely made judgments and classifications and acted upon them, believing that what I observed and heard was how the situation occurred.

One of my employees was extremely bright and lacked a college degree. I gave him a chance because I could tell his work ethic occurred during the interview as very high and his skill set raw, but manageable. After hiring him, I noticed that he was very slow to respond to my emails and when my requests required him to attach a document of any kind, there was no response. I began to judge the employee as lazy and question his work ethic.

With all my "wisdom" in hand, I confronted the person and told him that his lack of response was not acceptable and was causing me and others problems. I planned to put him on a program and manage him off the team.
That is, until I heard the truth: he didn't know how to use e-mail. Instead, he was using a feature in the word processing application to send an open document through e-mail

without opening the e-mail client. He did not know how to attach a document straight from e-mail.

The language in my mind was that he was a "lazy employee." When I used that language, I believed it and acted upon it. Had I been more mindful and only observed what was occurring, my language would have been different: "He isn't attaching documents I've requested." Perhaps I simply would have asked him
"Why?"

CHANGING LANGUAGE

When I began running peer boards with Vistage International, a leading provider of private executive peer boards, the business owners and executives I coached all updated each other on their progress against their plans using a 1 – 10 linear progression scale. Since 10 was the highest or best, then 1 was perceived as low. The subjective judgment built in was that people needed to get themselves up to 10.

Guess what happened? Some people were always checking in with "top" scores. After a while, others who were using the scale to communicate more accurately to the board began to abandon that effort and check-in using higher numbers. After 12 months, the scale had no relation to life.

My intuition told me that not everyone was having as good a life as they were claiming to be living. I then gave them a stress point exercise which helped them identify and communicate stresses in their lives. Once the results were discussed with the group, I turned back to the check-in board and asked them why their scores weren't reflecting reality.

Their answers were what you'd expect: even the security and safety of a private board with no competitors and confidentiality agreements in place could not overcome the power of language to communicate judgment. None of them wanted to check-in using the linear scale because its progressive and regressive elements created a sense of success or failure and judgment.

THE CHURP MODEL

From that experience, I created the CHURP model. It is a way to communicate situations in the neutral "observation" position. My boards made some tweaks and improvements to my original draft, and it is

Plan code	C	H	U	R	P
Key	Unexpected Change *Observing investigating*	Needs Help *Team is on it*	Urgent *Discuss with board today*	Redirect *Planned re-direction*	On Plan *Monitoring managing*
Description	Exceeded plan, market disruption, staff challenge, etc. that may affect the original plan	Product issues, customer issues, etc.. that may affect the original plan	Rapid change of events from plan, such as sudden growth, customer loss, lawsuit, etc.	Strategic decision by the stakeholders to redirect the company to a new plan	Growth, capital, cash management, product development are all on plan

presented here for your benefit. As you can see, there is no notion of success or failure in this tool. Situations are simply represented as they occur to the individual reporting on them. We can also map out the reporting more quickly on the double helix model.

In the illustration below, we're using the "top" line to represent the plans we've made. These are business plans, health plans, anything we intend to do in life and set expectations and intent toward.

When we are on plan, the CHURP method communicates that notion with a "P," for on plan. It just is. When events start to take us off plan slightly, we can communicate that with an "H" for help. Help, in the context of my boards, means they get to discuss the situation with each other and get different perspectives. If you're using this with your employees, the same scenario rings true.

When situations beyond our control take us off plan, a "C" is communicated and placed on the connecting rod. This "change" is an event that took us to another reality we didn't foresee.

At times, you will see situations that prompt you to change your plan. Believe it or not, I've seen many people acknowledge changing conditions and refuse to redirect their plan just because they did not want to look like a "bad" planner to others.

In the venture-backed world of companies, this happens all too often. Young entrepreneurs, emboldened by funding and the new title of CEO, believe the only way to prove themselves is to stick to a plan. This nonsense is often described as "bold leadership." Rather than changing trajectory, they drive the company off a cliff. Boards step in and fire the CEO. What the board—and employees—want is not arrogance disguised as leadership but rather a leader humble enough to redirect plans when necessary to meet the stated objective.

When you choose to change your plan, the CHURP model calls that a "redirect" or "R." R's, like their C counterparts, are also placed on the second line of the double helix.

For urgent changes that need immediate attention, the letter "U" is communicated. There's no shame in having a pressing issue to discuss with your business or life coach, boss, board or best friend. We all have issues that are urgent.

Mapping out the CHURP model on the double helix shows how life does unfold.

This chart displays a real-world revenue example. The blue

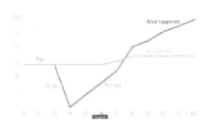

line is the original plan, and the red line shows what happened over 12 quarters. As you can see, life unfolded on a plan for three quarters and then took a

significant
dip in the fourth. The event that happened: all revenue was lost due to circumstances beyond their control. We model that event with a "C" for change. Emotionally, the event was painful. However, my client could stay at the neutral position and not judge themselves as failures. The clarity received from neutral allowed them to redirect their efforts

in an entirely different field—with results that exceeded their original 36-month plan.

The graph above took just the financial piece of my client's plan and modeled it. He recovered, redirected and ended up in a better place.

Shifts in language are what can take a miserable situation and allow it to occur hopeful or make a positive situation occur ominously.

Think of the Rev. Martin Luther King Jr.'s famous "I have a Dream" speech. For millions of Americans of all colors, the situation of the late 1950s and early 1960s was filled with segregation, rights deprivation and isolation. It occurred as perpetually hopeless. And then King, through his words, changed the way America occurred from a permanently racist society to one that had the structures and an inherent belief in freedom of equality that could enable anyone to rise and effect change. And rise he did. He boldly stated a vision that allowed people to see where they were as a launch pad to where they could be.

EXERCISE 4:

Use the situation you've referenced in the last four exercises and complete the activity below.

- How is the situation occurring now?
- How could the situation be in the future?
- Describe the situation using future-based language.

For instance, "I have an employee who does not follow the sales process, which diminishes my visibility into sales and makes managing the company more arduous than I believe it should be" then becomes: "I currently have an employee who does not follow the sales process, which diminishes my visibility into sales and makes managing the company more arduous than I believe it should be. I'm going to use this employee to discover what, if anything, is wrong with the process, add additional requirements and create a smoother running operation that will allow me to hire and ramp sales people more quickly and achieve greater profitability through the increased, consistent visibility I will achieve."

Consider:

1. Since you first described your situation in Exercise 1, how does it now occur?
1. How do you feel about the situation?
2. Has anything other than your language changed yet?
3. How will you consider using the Three Laws of Performance?
4. How do you think they will help you transform situations and the actions you take?

CHOOSING TO SEE THINGS DIFFERENTLY
REQUIRES A CHANGE IN LANGUAGE

Remember the double helix? When the bottom strand of the helix is acknowledged, we then can more readily disown judgment-based language and own our responsibility to move forward in a new creative way. If events take us off the top strand and down to the second, did we fail? The answer is no, of course. We simply ended up somewhere we didn't plan to be.

We call events that put us on the bottom strand "Changes." These are things that happen entirely outside our control. We cannot and should not chastise ourselves for changes to our plan dictated by bad luck, divine intervention or random chance. Whatever source you ascribe to the event, you at least know it wasn't you.

When a change occurs, we then take ownership of our responsibility to continue to march toward our goal, albeit on a different course. We can take a moment and assess where we are and how we can move from our current state forward toward our outcome. Because events are neutral and can happen independent of each other, we aren't so bothered that what we did last quarter didn't get us where we expected to be this quarter.

We ask ourselves these questions:

1. Where am I now with my desired outcome?
2. How did I get here, off my plan? Were there indicators I missed?
3. Is "here" a place for growth?
4. Is the path I built to get to my outcome still the correct path or is it better to redirect my efforts any other way to achieve my desired result?

Case Study: THE POWER OF LANGUAGE

One of my coaching clients had two major events unfold in the same quarter: 1) they *failed* to meet their quarterly EBITDA (earnings before interest, taxes, deductions and amortization) goals and 2) learned that four major customers may not renew their contracts with their company.

Here's how our conversation unfolded:

CEO: We failed to meet our profitability targets last quarter and, unrelated to that, I learned this week that four of our major accounts are now up for review. We may lose them.

ME: Let's look at each event separately. First, your profitability goals were not met.

CEO: Yes, that's right. We needed to be at 5 percent; we were at 2.5 percent.

Me: Okay. How are you reacting to that news?

CEO: I'm not happy, and I communicated that to my team, and we're taking measures to get back on plan.

Me: So, you are confident that your plan is something your business can achieve?

CEO: Yes, of course. That's why I wrote the plan.

Me: But your company didn't meet the plan. It's somewhere else.

CEO: Right, I get what you're saying. But a company needs a plan and goals to drive toward. Without that, we'll never hit anything.

Me: Okay. Let's talk about those four customers.

CEO: Yes, there were internal employee changes at those customers' companies, and the new people in charge are reviewing all vendors and will likely negotiate us down—again.

Me: Several unrelated events are occurring. Let's not consider any one of them failures or assume that getting back to plan is the right thing for the company right now. Let's just look at where we are as changes that occurred that may or may not be out of your control. Employee changes at your major accounts are certainly out of your control.

CEO: Okay, sure. We are at 2.5 percent profit, and we planned to be at 5 percent, and four customers may leave us or at least negotiate us down.

Me: Other than price, what other competitive advantages does your company have that might allow it to keep the business without being price-pressured?

CEO: None—in that area. It's a commodity service. We compete on price. That's it. In this other division, we have a lot of advantages and higher profitability— around 10 percent.

Me: Let me reflect what I'm hearing. Your profits didn't meet plan, and you are preparing to lower your profit margins to keep four customers in your commodity, price-war exposed business unit and expecting management to double net income to 5 percent by next quarter.

CEO: Yes, that's correct.

Me: Given what I just re-stated, did your company fail to meet plan or could the plan be faulty?

CEO: Yes, I get what you're saying. If I keep those customers—insist on keeping those customers—they'll further pressure margins. The reality of the situation is that we'll need to double our cost reduction plan to meet net income targets, but keeping those customers may reduce net income by half a point. It certainly wouldn't increase it.

Me: Right. So, have you failed or are you and your company exactly where it should be?

CEO: It occurs that we are where we need to be. Keeping those customers doesn't make sense for the business if they continue to squeeze our profitability. Me: Tell me about the other business unit with 10 percent profit margins. What would it take to grow that margin contribution to something significant enough to influence overall net income?

CEO: Cash. We have cash.

Me: *Silence. I just wait for the executive to connect all the dots.*

CEO: Okay. Here's what we need to consider: 1) The plan was wrong, not my team; 2) The business is flawed because it is overly reliant on the commodity business for revenue; 3) keeping those four customers at all costs—may cost us too much. We need to do a thorough profit and loss audit on them before choosing whether to keep them or let them go, and 4) a better path to hitting our profitability objectives may be to invest in this smaller division because it's not a commodity sale and
has much higher net incomes.

Me: That's a much different strategy than the one you described when the meeting began. What made the difference?

CEO: Well, you forced me to look at our results, not as a failure to achieve, but rather events that needed to be investigated. Ultimately, it seems the plan is to blame because the company is out of balance. Any new plan to hit profitability targets must consider growing the profitable business units while winding ourselves out of the commodity business we've been doing for 20 years.

WHAT JUST HAPPENED?

In the real-world example above, the CEO changed the way he viewed the plan. Did you notice the shift?

Starting perspective: Initially, the CEO believed he failed to meet the plan and had communicated that to the management team, pushing them to get back onto plan. Transition: After removing the word "failure," the CEO then was open to the concept that perhaps the plan, not his team, was not realistic.

New vantage point: He then acknowledged that the company is on a different line (not the linear progression he planned) and that this new place is likely exactly where the company should be, given its current structure.

New vision (R for Redirection): Once acknowledging that he was at a new point, he then changed the way the four low-margin, high revenue customers occurred to him. His mind then went into rapid-fire mode, generating the radically new idea that he should strongly consider growing the small high-margin business at the expense of the commodity business they were in for 20 years—and possibly fire the four low-margin customers.

Positive energy hits the executive team: The CEO went back to the executive team with the new perspective. They hadn't failed. Situations occurred that prevented the plan from being met, and therefore analysis of a new strategy was needed as a result. The goals were noble and still the target. The team was now given the freedom to explore creative avenues to increase profitability that no one had considered previously. In the linear progression model, the only possibility of achievement is the next progression, which was net income of 5 percent.

By considering two lines and events as neutral, the CEO was able to envision a net income target of 10 percent— if the company dissolved the low-margin, high commodity business over time.

The ideas and possibilities are always available to us. Negative language and narrow, wrong views of how events and plans unfold put blinders on us which force us to see only the plan generated by our will, depriving us of full use of the creative mind we're given.

IS THE PLAN EVER RIGHT?

Some have argued that this way of thinking may always lead to the conclusion that plans or goals are wrong if not met, as opposed to the institution being wrong in trying to achieve them.

First, unless we are discussing moral values (which we aren't), there is no "right" or "wrong." With planning and goal-setting, both just "are what they are," not right or wrong.

Only you know if your plan is aligned to company needs and achievable. Company "needs" vary from company to company.

CEOs in publicly traded companies need to deliver consistency in revenue to investors. The plans they communicate to the company and public are usually going to be less than the CEO believes the company can achieve. Over-reaching is punished by the market if that over-reach wasn't met.

CEOs of venture-backed companies are pushed to create plans with rapid revenue growth often forecasted at 100 percent plus, year-over-year. These executives are damned if they do create such a plan and damned if they don't hit it.

If you feel your plan is achievable and it wasn't achieved, it still should not be considered a failure because only available plans can be attained. In other words, the question to ask yourself is not how to get your team to achieve what occurs to you as achievable, but rather what is going on in my company that rendered this plan unachievable?

This small shift in focus may lead you to discover a sales person who has been sleeping on the job for three quarters or other issues within the company that rendered it incapable of executing to plan. Fix those things, and the company will then be able to perform as you thought it should have been able to all along.

Your plan, therefore, is simply a way to test your assumptions by seeing if the company and your employees are as capable as they are occurring.

LANGUAGE TRANSFORMS SITUATIONS

FUTURE-BASED LANGUAGE TRANSFORMS HOW SITUATIONS OCCUR TO PEOPLE. —THE THIRD LAW OF PERFORMANCE.[4]

---

[4] Steve Zaffron and David Logan, *The Three Laws of Performance: Rewriting the Future of Your Organization and Your Life*. (San Francisco:

We've already covered how removing failure-based language and other judgmental adjectives from your lexicon can release anxiety and free your mind to think more creatively through situations.

Now, let's add the third law, from the book *The Three Laws of Performance*. Future-based language has the power to transform any situation, regardless of how dire it looks, into an opportunity for growth that creates positive energy and attracts people to you and your vision.

Consider the Rev. Martin Luther King Jr. He had a dream that one day all people, while created equally, would actually be treated equally. His famous "I Have a Dream" speech turned a permanent oppressive social construct into a situation that, for the first time in U.S. history, began to look temporary. His future-based language motivated millions of people of all races and, over time, equal rights became law. Society still has not achieved his dream, but neither has it stopped trying to get there.

President John F. Kennedy envisioned the U.S. putting a human on the moon before all but a few scientists at NASA believed it was even possible. This audacious dream defined his presidency because it reignited the pioneering spirit that has defined Americans for hundreds of years. And yes, a human made it to the moon.

Josse Bass, 2009), 68.

The famous King of Israel, Solomon wrote in Proverbs 29:18: "Where there is no vision, the people perish." Vision is future-based language.

REASONS WE LOSE OUR VISION: THE CURSE OF THE FIRST

Stagnant growth, lack of innovation, declining creativity, apathy and complacency all stem from lack of vision. Executives who at one time rocketed their companies to market leadership often lose their ability to dream once their first vision is attained.

The company descends into slow or anemic growth as the instinct to preserve a market position takes over, driven by the fear of losing it. The results are predictable: growth slows to the pace of the market (which is no growth), then falls into growth rates lower than the market is growing (loss of market share), and then eventually the company's position as a market leader is overcome by another, more visionary business leader.

I call this situation the "curse of the first." It's a strange human trait that has us risking everything to create something amazing and then when we've attained it, we transform into a low-risk, self-preservation mode that is counter productive to self-preservation.

THE CURSE OF THE PAST

In many cases, changes in environments that put people off plan are catalysts for a harmful belief that futurebased *anything* is pointless. We simply stop believing we can change our circumstances because our past has "proven" that we lack the capability to dream accurately.

The past and future exist only in your mind. You can't go back to the past, so it doesn't exist, and you can't leap into the future. While our logic and training use past performance as indicators of future results, the reality is that past and future have no correlation to each other. Dr. King believed that the past had no influence over his ability to create a new future, which allowed him to work unencumbered in his present.

THE PRESENT SITUATION LOOKS IMPOSSIBLE TO ESCAPE

It is entirely possible to believe that the past has no power over the future and still not be able to generate or move forward on a vision because your present occurs as confining.

Working parents can become so overwhelmed with financial stress, kids' activities and job responsibilities that any transitions toward a desired outcome different than the present may occur as impossible or perhaps "foolish" to consider. Parents that stay home full time can find themselves in a position that occurs even more untenable. During the last 20 years, technology has transformed our world much more quickly and dramatically than it had in previous generations.

Many find that the talents they had before leaving the workforce are completely archaic today and have little market value. The option to reinvent oneself, especially when coupled with financial constraints, can seem impossible.

WE FEAR GETTING WHAT WE WANT

I've seen this reality many times with employees. There are some who dream of moving into management and choose to use every excuse possible not actually to get there. Some dream of starting their companies or working for a start-up, but opt to avoid those paths when they present themselves.

Common to these two categories of people is a fear that they'll get what they want and won't like it when they do. Life in its current form is comfortable, and quarterbacking from the couch creates an illusion for themselves and others that they want leadership. However, the fear of getting what they want is conning them into staying in the life they say they want to change.

HOW TO GET A VISION FOR YOUR FUTURE

The first steps toward creating your vision are to identify and remove limiting beliefs, realize that the past has no correlation to the future and then change the way your dreams occur to you from impossible to possible. The final step is to write your vision down on paper using future-based language. When we use future-based language, the way our present occurs to us will transform. You're going to try this very soon. But first, let's look at one other law that will be working for your benefit.

It's called *The Law of Attraction.*

THE LAW OF ATTRACTION

The Law of Attraction: The Basics of the Teachings of Abraham, by Esther and Jerry Hicks, describes an abstract concept some believe is programmed into the universe. The idea is simple: when we add intention and positive emotion to our thoughts, we will attract that which we want. According to the theory, the laws are amoral. We attract what consumes us, whether good or bad. What we declare in language has a direct correlation to what we receive in reality.[5]

When we focus on the present tasks at hand—whether running our business or doing anything else—the situation we are in occurs to us a certain way and, like we already learned, it first occurs in language.

When that language becomes a belief, then the Laws of Attraction kick into high gear. Let's say your business has grown to $10 million and revenue has been flat for three years. The goals and ambitions you associate with higher revenues and profits are stuck, too.

---

[5] Concepts in this section are taken from: Esther and Jerry Hicks, *The Law of Attraction: The Basics and Teachings of Abraham* (Carlsbad, CA: Hay House, 2010).

Eventually, your mind begins to conclude that certain things may simply not be achievable logically. After trying to break the revenue logjam with no success, those attempts start to occur as evidence that your business is not capable of growing beyond its current state and the dreams you attached to higher levels of achievement are not feasible. Evidence builds into an argument that, when unopposed, forms a belief system.

At this point, you're almost toast. Your mind acts in agreement with beliefs. It will start to solve only problems that challenge the idea that your company can only be a $10 million company. Issues that arise now will occur as threats to the current status. The survival instinct kicks in, and we can begin managing in survival mode. When revenue and profits dip, the brain solves by advising us to cut expenses. With expenses cut, employees now start to believe that the company's future is jeopardized. Because it occurs this way to them, they start to underperform and leave. And the cycle continues as fear-based management only has one outcome: disaster.

Per the concept of *the Law of Attraction*, the energy behind the belief attracted the law into action and the results became what we believed them to be. We attracted what we thought to be possible. When our belief is negative and fueled by anxiety and fear, we attract negative consequences—like a downward spiral to disaster.

THIS LAW IS VERY HARD TO CONCEPTUALIZE, I GET IT.

114

Personally, I've always had a problem with this concept because I am a very pragmatic, evidence-driven decision maker. Faith in anything—especially myself and others—is an ongoing challenge for me because my natural tendency is to view situations as evidence pointing to some conclusion I need to make. While I'm not convinced that there is a mystical force that delivers to us what we want or believes we are capable of attracting or achieving, I am confident that our minds work in a way the Law attributes to metaphysics.

We become what consumes us. This pattern is true for everything. If pornography consumes us, we'll become sex addicts. If we are consumed with not paying taxes, we may eventually cheat on our taxes or engage in fraud. If we are consumed with greed, we'll end up stealing and cheating our way to wealth. If we are obsessed with the belief that our situation can't be changed, then it never will.

Are we attracting some force to deliver those things into our lives or is our mind an incredible machine that simply gives us more of what it believes we want and finds opportunities to make that happen? I don't know.

What I do know, however, is that since writing my personal Outcome Statement, reading it daily, believing it can happen and directing positive thoughts of hope and achievement toward my desired outcome, I've begun to achieve it—quickly. I am attracting into my life what my Outcome Statement desires (so far).

Here are a few reasons I believe my plans are now manifesting in my life in ways they never did previously:

- My Outcome Statement uses future-based language. It is written in the future, which makes my past irrelevant and my present occurs as a means to that future, not a perpetual prison. My desires and goals are only 36 months ahead. In the past, I dreamed of what I'd one day do if I had some degree of time and money on my hands. My business would IPO or I'd write books—items like that which were too far removed in time for me to believe they could happen. Without the belief, I put little energy behind the desires.

- My goals and outcomes are very precise. In the past, my desires were not as specific as they needed to be and therefore occurred as ambiguous. Ambiguity only manifests as ambiguity and doesn't generate an apparent problem our brains can work to solve.
  Ambiguity is the problem.

- I have changed the way my current situation occurs. The previous goal-setting usually failed because I believed that my desired outcomes had to logically progress from the way my current situation happened to me. In the past, I didn't change the way the situation occurred. If I believed my situation was hopeless, then the vision of my future happened as unreachable. I can't get "there" if I don't believe I'll ever be able to leave "here."

- I read my Outcome Statement every day. The world's most successful people understand their goals every single day. This exercise keeps the game posts in sight always. Focusing on the end game allows us to see current challenges in the context of the future. With the goal in mind, we can evaluate more clearly and objectively the tasks we choose to invest our time and resources to complete.

- My mind is now consciously and subconsciously programmed to observe the world around it in the context of my dreams.

The sixth point is perhaps the most important because it is the result of points 1 – 5. When we continue to focus on the first five elements, we are telling our mind to "go make it happen." When it is aware of what we want, it notices things around us that may help us get to that outcome quickly.

To achieve success in 12 quarters, you don't need to believe in the metaphysical. You do, however, need to apply the principles those laws clearly establish.

Focus on what is right and positive in your life. Seriously. Turn the news off or get your information from sources with a penchant for pragmatic, rather than negative, reporting.

1. Do not dwell on the negative. For example, if you're continually strapped for cash, do not say to yourself, "I'm always cash-strapped," but rather say, "I have enough cash now and will have more than enough cash in the future." This will get your mind out of the mire and will program it to find ways to make that statement and belief a reality.

2. Let your Word be spoken out loud through language. Read your Outcome Statement out loud every day. Let your mind hear it repeatedly until it becomes your belief.

3. Believe that what you wish to achieve can be accomplished. Don't take this to a natural conclusion. Doing so will cause your mind to interject doubts, which create arguments that then destroy our ability to believe. If your outcome in 12 quarters is to have four weeks of vacation and a Porsche in the garage, you may end up with the choice to take four weeks of vacation and ultimately decide to buy a Lamborghini rather than a Porsche. The point of believing is not that your ultimate choice to change your outcome will be removed but rather that you will be working to create situations that allow that outcome to be achieved if you so desire.

4. Work. None of the laws presented in this book are magic wands; you must commit each day and every day to do what is necessary to achieve your outcome.

APPLYING YOUR NEW LANGUAGE BY MAKING AGREEMENTS WITH YOURSELF

As we wrap up this section on language, we're going to look at the agreements/commitments you must make to yourself to make your outcome a reality. It's not enough just to understand and believe the concepts you've read; they must be put into action.

Your word brings the process; keeping it drives it forward. *The Four Agreements: A Practical Guide to Personal Freedom* by Don Miguel Ruiz, identifies these four keys to success:

- Be impeccable with your word.
- Don't take anything personally.
- Don't make assumptions.
- Always do your best.[6]

AGREEMENT 1: BE IMPECCABLE WITH YOUR WORD.

The first agreement is by far the hardest to achieve and the most important ingredient to your success.

When you embark on your 12-quarter plan, you will be making a promise to yourself to begin building the outcome you desire.

---

[6] Don Miguel Ruiz, *The Four Agreements* (San Rafael, CA: Amber-Allen Publishing, 2010). I think the year should be 1997

119

The people that are most successful in life are those who keep their word to themselves. Pick any leader—from Mother Teresa and Gandhi to Bono of U2 or any President of the United States—and they will acknowledge their success was dependent on their ability to keep their promises to themselves, first.

If you currently do not value your word, then you'll need to change the way your word occurs to yourself immediately.

- What you say you will do, do you must.
- When you don't do what you say you will, your word becomes powerless.
- When your word has no power to you, it occurs as something weak and not worthy of your time.
- When it happens weak, your mind will value your word as it suggests—not as a command to act.
- Suggestions are often not acted upon.
- Lack of actions creates a lack of results.
- Lack of results is used as evidence against your plan.
- Evidence that the plan isn't working becomes a belief that it is not achievable.
- When the plan occurs as not possible, you are likely to say it is not feasible.
- When you say it is not achievable, you will not do it.
- When you don't do it, you will stay where you are.

When you are impeccable with your word, first to yourself, naturally you will start occurring as such to others. How many issues do we have today because we simply don't believe people will do what they say they will?

AGREEMENT 2: DON'T TAKE ANYTHING PERSONALLY.

According to *The Four Agreements*, nothing other people do is because of you, and it is because of themselves and the way they view situations. Of course, we can elicit reactions by the way we act and therefore, at times, become complicit and need to take ownership in our contribution to the way someone reacts to us.

Quite often, our egos tend to believe certain comments and actions from others or situations are directly attributed to or targeted at us. This "ownership" of situations is the third step to processing conditions after we observe and classify them.

When you choose not to take situations personally, your perspective will change dramatically, and you'll be better equipped to rise back up to the first neutral position that is observing events and seeing what is there.

During the next 12 quarters, commit to yourself to stay in observation mode as much as possible. All you can control is the way you react when such situations arise. You can't make people laugh or cry; those are their choices. Even what they think of you is only 50 percent in your control. The other party owns their reaction to your actions. When marching through your 36-month plan, this agreement to yourself not to take anything personally is crucial for two important reasons.

- <u>You are not your plan.</u> Your plan is going to be bold and includes stretch objectives you've likely never considered possible. If we were working together and I was your business coach, I'd insist on such goals being included. Hitting all the stretch objectives isn't the point of having them on the plan.
Missing a few of them will not reflect who you are, although it may reveal strengths you have or areas for growth. Don't take the plan personally.
Remember, it's not a prophecy.

- <u>Changes you make to your business may disrupt some relationships.</u> One of the substantial challenges of owning a business is the care and responsibility owners feel toward their employees. Long-term hires can start to occur much like family. Quite often, my clients realize that their plan can't be achieved with the team they have. It took one of my clients nearly a year to remove a long-term employee, not because the employee was fighting the change, but rather the business owner had a very hard time getting to the mental state necessary to make a move. They were taking it personally, in part because they had stories in their heads that the employee they wanted to remove would react negatively, attack them and walk away from the relationship. None of that happened when the move was finally made.

AGREEMENT 3: DON'T MAKE ASSUMPTIONS.

The financial models for your plan will be based on assumptions. In fact, your entire 36-month plan assumes you will be alive to complete it. Those assumptions, of course, are not what this agreement considers. Put another way, not making assumptions is a promise to yourself to a) watch what stories your mind forms about situations and b) test those stories before believing them and acting upon them.

Most problems business owners encounter are caused by acting on assumptions without doing the research to prove or disprove them. We act upon our assumptions because we believe they are truth. In many cases, business owners get into trouble with what seem to be the tiniest issues that could easily have been prevented. Here's a fun list of the most numerous assumptions I've encountered:

- I hired a new employee and just assumed they knew how to do this most basic task.
- When I sent the attachment, I thought he'd open it and respond.
- I just assumed my partner was on the same page with me, but he's not.
- I assumed my vendor was in good financial shape. Now they've gone under, and I can't source this product.
- I've had this customer for years; I guess I just assumed they'd continue to use my company.
- When the engineer told me the core product would be completed on time, I assumed it included all the features. Apparently, their definition of "core" and

mine aren't aligned, and now I've lost precious time to market.

- When I struck a 50/50 partnership deal, I assumed my partner would continue to carry 50 percent of the load, so I didn't build in provisions to protect me if the reverse was proven.

QUESTIONS, NOT ASSUMPTIONS

Take a moment and list as many assumptions as you can think of that you are currently making, each on a separate sheet of paper.

For each assumption you listed, some questions need to be asked. Before we can get to a mental space where our mind shifts from knowing to questioning, we must assume that we don't know what we think we do.

This was difficult to do for business owners because so many of the blind spots that surprise us fall into areas of our expertise. We assume that because we know something, someone else will as well. Here's a list of standard questions that help test our blind spots and lead to areas of discovery that protect us from the perils of assumptive leadership.

- What do I believe is true about_____?
- What information do I have that makes me think this is true?
- Does my employee have the same information?
- What gaps in the information do I perceive? •
  In what ways can I collect the information?
  If I have all the information, will that prove my assumption or are there other data points I still need?

-
- How often should I test this assumption to make sure it is still true?
- Do I have a process or standard operating procedure in place for this assumption?
- How expensive to my business would this assumption be if it proved to be untrue?
- What management decisions have I made under this assumption?

AGREEMENT 4: ALWAYS DO YOUR BEST.

When I first read this agreement, I laughed a little bit. It sounded somewhat childish and was, in fact, something I told my children all too many times (in their opinion). The more I reflected on it, however, the greater the importance this agreement began to have in my life and in the way I occurred to myself.

- If I always did my best, I couldn't judge myself if the results that materialized were less than my expectations.
- If I always did my best and events outside my control took me off my course, then I was less anxious about my abilities.
- If I always did my best, then times when I was not true to my word would be fewer.
  If I always did my best, then I could expect the same from others without feeling or occurring as hypocritical.
- My best is not defined as perfect. The quest for perfection of effort and results seems moot and almost silly. No one is

- perfect and complete results are impossible to realize. Doing my best is the highest metric I can achieve.
- If I always do my best, then I am allowing myself to relinquish control.

Case Study: Asia-Pacific Director

The last point is a significant mind shift that has an immediate ability to reduce stress.

In one of my coaching sessions, a mid-level director said she was under a tremendous amount of stress at work. She managed Asia-Pacific manufacturing for a US-based client. Her manufacturer in China was missing deadlines and had suddenly stopped responding to her calls and those of her company's president based in the United States, to whom she reported. She felt a grave responsibility to get this manufacturer to respond and get back on schedule.

This is a terrible scenario to coach for a few reasons:

Product managers are the world's greatest orchestrators of processes and people. The symphony of internal employees, vendors, manufacturers, consultants and quality engineers usually do not report to them directly. Lack of direct authority to influence the behavior of others through rewards or dangling carrots creates a severe power gap that the world's best directors—and she is among the world's best—overcome with their unique ability to prod, cajole and motivate others.

-

- Since she is one of the best in her class, she reported directly to the president of the company and was essential to their leadership team. And yet she only had one direct report. Her talent, thoroughness, and attention to detail left no stone unturned and me with few options toward which to coach. She had done everything she could do. There wasn't anything else she could make possible, an attempt that would change the behavior of the now belligerent manufacturer. She was a magician who had driven people, and she didn't control from three continents to get a product almost to market four months faster than anyone else could have done.

She had done her best, which was better than anyone else I know could have done. And her best wasn't "good enough." How do I tell someone of this caliber that if she "did her best," she could give herself grace?

I couldn't do it. Like other professionals who aren't satisfied with their best if their best only achieves the worst results, this fourth agreement would have occurred as simplistic and patronizing.

And yet, it is anything but simplistic and patronizing. It's freeing. Rather than telling her, I opted for an exercise to show her what she already knew and yet was not able to fully believe or embrace during this stressful period. The task was simple:

1. Draw a line down the middle of a sheet of paper.
2. Label the first column: "What I can control."
3. Label the second column: "What I can't control."
4. Complete the columns, writing whatever comes to mind (much like brainstorming).
5. Evaluate the "What I can control" column and make notes on everything in that column that you missed, didn't accomplish thoroughly or feel could be revisited to achieve different results.

Not surprisingly, apart from the facetious mention of breaking through the front door of the manufacturing plant owner's home, there was nothing left that she controlled for her to do. She had, in truth, done her best.

It's important to mention that much of our stress is also created when we do not properly set expectations for our performance to others. In this case, because she is a professional, she was smart enough not to promise her president that she could "deliver" the product. Her original commitment to him was to be the best in her industry.

She had met that commitment and, because of her clarity at the project's inception, was not under unreasonable pressure from her superior. To him, she occurred as someone who had delivered what she promised; it was evident the manufacturer was to blame and not her.

The next step in the exercise was for her to look internally at her emotions. It would have been much easier to control her anxiety now that she could see what she already knew to be true: that she had done her best.

- She could not control the actions of the plant owner and could not be responsible for them.
- Her president did not feel she had failed or was failing.
- The only possible consequences of her best efforts were that her company was in a stellar position to seek retribution from the manufacturer—and that's an excellent position for future negotiations.
- This 30-minute exercise changed the way her situation occurred to her dramatically:
    - o False: "I can get them to communicate if I only try harder."
    - o Truth: "I can't control people. It is his responsibility to contact us now."
    - o Truth: "Because I did my best, my president is not retributive toward me."

- o Truth: "Because I did my best, my president is now in an adamant position to exact retributive concessions from this manufacturer which may drive down costs and increase our margins."
- Affirming Statement: "I will no longer allow myself to feel anxious. I'm a hero, the best in my profession and worth more than my company's president is currently paying me."

Meditation: The Power of Stillness

For most of us, the idea of stilling our mind occurs as a daunting task with little real-world practical benefits. Meditation is the intentional, yet paradoxical, practice of clearing the mind for a space of time. It's paradoxical because clearing the mind takes active involvement of the mind to be still and control, then tamp or at least slow down the volume and pace of random thoughts that it generates. There are many different practices of meditation available. Some promote relaxation while others build energy.

There's plenty of scientific evidence now that describes how meditation increases serotonin levels, reduces anxiety and allows the mind space to think more clearly.
I won't cover any of that evidence, though, as it's easily found online.

Another benefit many CEOs and executives find with regular meditation is the ability to think more creatively. Personally, I found that after meditating, my mind generates very creative solutions to big problems I was considering and small issues that occurred as important were suddenly put into perspective.

131

Both these phenomena reduced stress and increased productivity and mental discipline throughout the day. Meditating on your Outcome Statement each morning—simply read it, repeat it in your mind and then sit still for 10 or 15 minutes—will clear your head of the daily tactical items for a few minutes and let your mind free its energy to solve the "problem" of creating your outcome.

Tom Cronin, a former money broker, felt meditation had such an impact on his life that he quit his high-stress job and founded The Stillness Project, which aims to inspire one billion people to meditate for at least 20 minutes each day.

There are many reasons more people don't meditate on a regular basis. One of the top reasons cited is a lack of time. Tom has found a way to overcome this objection by reframing his day into 72 twenty-minute blocks of time. For Tom, spending just two of these 72 blocks in stillness reaps innumerable benefits. And besides, he still has 70 blocks of time to do whatever else he chooses. Prior to starting his meditation practice, he would fill those blocks with work, drugs, alcohol and other distractions to find fulfillment. Once he started meditating, he began to change his lifestyle. His personal success compelled him to start teaching and building The Stillness Project in his spare time.

"Once I started meditating, I noticed that my relationships began to improve, my anxiety was reduced, my wealth began to grow and my work life balance gradually came into congruence with a healthier lifestyle," he said.

"I spend just two blocks of 20 minutes out of the 72 twenty-minute blocks available each day 'being' rather than 'doing. — Tom Cronin, Founder of the Stillness Project

In addition to meditation, Tom has three other secrets to goal achievement.

1. Meditation
2. Operate free from stress
3. Have fun
4. Don't go it alone

Operate Stress-Free. The number two priority after meditation is to operate from a state of being that is free from as much stress as possible, per Cronin. Stress destroys our ability to see clearly what is happening.
Only when we can see clearly can we make the best decisions. Meditation, of course, helps control and reduce the anxieties of running a business.

Have Fun. "I see so many business leaders who are stressed and grumpy all the time. It's because their life is out of balance, which only leads to the continued cycle of being stressed, grumpy and making less than optimal decisions. People should have fun distractions to be successful. It's what keeps the mind fresh and energized."

When we get to the end of our life and we have thirty minutes left, do we want to think: "Wow, I had a very successful business, but I wonder how my children are doing?" he mused.

To his point, several years ago, I met with a very successful CEO in Silicon Valley for dinner. With a net worth of more than $100 million and plenty of peer and academic notoriety for her achievements, it would occur as if she had it all. She paid $1 million for a Kentucky Derby winning stallion, and the life-size painting of it that hung in her home came in at $100,000. Her house was built from 300-year-old barn wood scoured from all over Europe. After a bottle of wine shared between us and a second on its way, she confessed the truth: she'd give it all away just to have a relationship with her children. She had worked constantly while they were young and now that they were adults, the relationship was so estranged that she rarely heard from them.

Sometimes what we think we want at the time isn't always what we really want. Without people around us to keep us in check, we may over-index on the business and lose sight of what matters to us.

Don't Go It Alone. Tom's fourth priority to goal achievement is to join with other people to help support the quest to create the desired outcome. The power of an ecosystem—whether that be a peer group, coaches or friends—is unmatched in its ability to foster accountability and drive results.

Application to Your 12-Quarter Plan

In the next chapter, you will begin to create your Outcome Statement—the vision of your life and how your business fits into it—that you will build over the next 12 quarters.

Take Tom's advice to heart. Still your mind before beginning the exercise and answering the questions, rid yourself of emotional stress, commit to having fun and build that into your plan and consider joining with others—either a coach or a peer board—to journey with you.

In my boards, we process topics not based on what is best for the business, but rather how the opportunity helps or hurts someone's drive toward their outcome.

One topic we discussed was a mergers and acquisitions. Buying a company was not on the CEO's plan, but an opportunity had arisen that he felt he needed to pursue to grow the business. His board, however, compared the opportunity to his Outcome Statement, which defined a life of less travel and more time with the family.

The conclusion of the board: The M&A opportunity was incongruent with the life the CEO was trying to build for himself. The CEO either needed to redefine his outcome or pass on the acquisition.

Even though the acquisition was a good, low-risk deal, his peer board advised against it because it would have doubled his travel and cut in half the time he currently spent with the family. There was no judgment from the board on how the CEO should live his life; they simply held him to the description of his future he created for himself.

After realizing that he had completely been distracted from his goal by the shiny object of fast growth, he decided to pass on the acquisition.

**BEHIND EVERY PROBLEM IS A QUESTION TRYING TO ASK ITSELF.
BEHIND EVERY QUESTION IS AN ANSWER TRYING TO BE REVEALED.
BEHIND EVERY ANSWER IS AN ACTION TRYING TO TAKE PLACE.
AND BEHIND EVERY ACTION IS A WAY OF LIFE TRYING TO BE BORN.
SO WHAT NEW WAY OF LIFE ARE YOU GOING TO GIVE BIRTH TO AND FOR HUMANITY?" --MICHAEL BECKWITH**

It's now time to put all the principles you've learned into action by creating your Outcome Statement.

This statement puts everything you've learned so far into an executable process that will change your trajectory. It also fuses the notions of "business" time and "personal" time into just "time."

Your Outcome Statement (OS) is the engine of your plan—the machine of your intention that propels you forward and becomes the rubric for decisions you will make during the next 36 months.

Many of the concepts you learned in the first part of this book come swiftly to bear when putting together this powerful, guiding statement. In the table below, you can see the laws, principles and biology that we've covered and their direct application within the Outcome Statement.

Case Study: Ken Thieneman

We met Ken earlier in this book, as the CEO who called this process a "life accelerator." Ken Thieneman is the 50-year-old president and founder of Thieneman Construction, in Westfield, roughly 10 miles north of downtown Indianapolis. Thieneman builds waste water treatment plants for cities and towns in the Midwest and brings in about $60 million in top line revenue per year with more than 100 employees.

Ken is a very goal-driven, high-energy executive with a penchant for details few others possess and a zest for life. After spending more than a decade growing his company from a folding table in his basement to where it is today, he felt he had hit a crossroads.

While business was good, it was stressful. He was carrying too much of the load, working 60- to 70-hour weeks, missing valuable time with the family and feeling that he was constantly stressed. He felt that much of his life was out of alignment.

Ken's first step to re-alignment was to join the Vistage executive peer board I was leading. Surrounding himself with other business owners exposed him to the reality that he was not alone and could if he chose, use the board as a cathartic and solutions-generating shoulder to lean on when needed.

His second step in his effort to re-calibrate his life was to build a strategic life and business plan using the process you're reading about in this book. He, along with 30 other CEOs and executives I coach, all began to reshape their world in just 12 quarters.

"When I first saw the Outcome Statement exercise, I was floored," he said. "I had always thought of my life as two separate buckets: work and personal. Work always got the biggest spend of my time, and I never felt that it could be any other way. Believing I could change all of that in just 12 quarters was highly energizing and was just what I needed."

Ken's approach to the Outcome Statement was unique, to say the least. Rather than planning a life with him in it in 12 quarters, he asked himself the morbid question few like to consider: "What if I planned my life as if I die in 12 quarters? How would I like to live the next 36 months and how can I shape my business to run without me by that time?"

While not the approach most takes, his logic was flawless: if he planned the world without him in it, then during the next 36 months, he'd focus on living a more balanced life and getting his company into a place where it could operate without him or be valuable enough to sell to its employees while also freeing his wife from having to run the company in case the worst happened. She had her own businesses to run and didn't want or need the headache of running one in a completely new industry to her.

When he reaches the end of his 12 quarters and is still alive, he'll have a company that's in great shape and all the options to either run it part time, sell it or continue to build it. What he wanted in 12 quarters was to be living a life that had plenty of time with the family and options for what to do with or how much to work in and on the business.

Options were something he felt he didn't have. Instead, he felt like he was "chained to the business" and wasn't fully embracing his power to choose a different course of
his life and, even more importantly, the ability to make that choice a reality. Ken lacked the tools to help him sift through the false stories in his head, design an integrated life and business plan of choices to make over 12 quarters and peer accountability to help him stay on track with the choices he intended to make.

As you begin the Outcome Statement process, you will notice the principles you've discovered in this book mashing together into one very clear and concise declarative statement for the life you will choose to live in 12 quarters. The table below describes the principles and how they are at work in the statement you will create.

Concept	Application
Changing Your Language	You will likely be changing the way individual goals and objectives occurred to you in the past, then having the new perspective arise in language, which will be written in the future as if it's already accomplished.

Removing Limiting Beliefs, Step 1.	Your OS is written as if it already occurred and needs to be very specific. You will then read your OS daily, thus reminding your mind to continually observe situations through the lens of where you will be in 12 quarters.
Fusing Life and Business	The OS mashes up your life and business buckets into one single statement that is your outcome. It will drive you to focus on you, first.
Inverting the Pendulum	The OS is designed to reset the Pendulum with you at the top. The pendulum will reset in 12 quarters, but your mindset will begin to change instantly.
Biology of the Brain	The OS is written to get through the gatekeeper of your mind by presenting it with an ideal that occurs as achievable and less painful than maintaining the status quo.

THINK NO FURTHER THAN 12 QUARTERS AHEAD

Three years is the optimum time frame for planning.
Five years is a bit too long for the mind to comprehend and more likely to be exposed to economic and political cycles than a three-year plan.

That said, financial planners tend to focus on long-term goals like retirement planning that's grounded in your ideals for life without work. That strategy is okay for a long-term, broader goal like "I want $5 million when I'm 65 so that I can have the lifestyle I want to lead."

If you have such a goal, keep it in mind when you focus on the next three years; don't abandon it. You will want to put the quarterly savings goals from your financial planner into the 12-quarter plan you are going to build.

PUT INTO PRACTICE WHAT YOU'VE LEARNED

The first question of the first exercise is likely going to derail you or get you started on the right path. It all depends on your willingness to give the principles you've learned an honest shot.

Let's walk through the first questions together.

"Describe the life you are living three years from today's date—what time of day are you stopping your business activities?"

FRAME YOUR MIND

First, don't look at the present as an indicator of the future. Whether you stop your business activities at 8 p.m. now has no correlation to when you will be stopping them three years from now.

Second, don't use the answer that seems most likely to be achieved. If it occurs as achievable now, it probably isn't that much of a stretch goal. Choose the answer that you want, even if it seems unachievable. As you do this, you will be changing the way the situation occurs, and you'll be doing it with language.

Last, be as specific with your answer as possible. If you want to stop doing business activities variably, depending on the day of the week, make sure you add that specificity. You'll be programming your brain to solve that problem.

Example: "The year is 2020, and I am stopping my business activities at 2 p.m. every Tuesday and Thursday and 6 p.m. every Monday, Wednesday and Friday."

BE BOLD

This isn't an exercise in mediocrity, so be bold with your plan and focus your thoughts and emotional energy at determining what it is that you want your life to look like in three years. If it doesn't occur as possible now, that's probably the answer you should write down.

VACATION TIME—MORE POWERFUL THAN YOU MAY THINK

When you get to this part of the plan, spend as much time on it as necessary. Don't rush into it. While it seems like a good statement, it is perhaps the single most significant problem you may solve if you aren't currently taking the amount of time off that'd you like.

Remember Curt, from the beginning of the book? He struggled to see the importance of vacation time to shape his business—until he pondered it carefully. In 18 years, he had not been able to take four contiguous weeks off from business activities. After some prodding, he finally added "four contiguous weeks in July" to his statement.

OUTCOME STATEMENT EXERCISE 1

DESCRIBE THE LIFE YOU ARE LEADING 3 YEARS FROM TODAY'S DATE.

1	What time of day are you stopping your business activities?
2	Who are you working for (self, the same employer as today, other)?
3	What job title do you have?
4	How many days did you travel the previous month?

5	How many direct reports do you have?
6	How many weeks of vacation are you planning?
7	How much money/savings /investments do you have socked away?
8	How is your health?
9	If you have children, how many of their activities are you planning to attend? (percentage—"all" may or may not be realistic)?
10	If you have a significant other, how many date nights per month are you having with them?
11	What top goals have you set for yourself and accomplished (personal, financial, relationship, health, recreation, possessions, and contribution)?
12	If you were granted three wishes to make any three goals come true, which three would you choose?

OUTCOME STATEMENT EXERCISE 2

DESCRIBE YOU, THE PERSON

1	What are your greatest passions and talents?

2	Titles, positions and wealth do not define you. What does? How do you want others to describe you in three years? Don't add titles, positions or wealth to the description.

OUTCOME STATEMENT EXERCISE 3

MAKE DECLARATIVE STATEMENTS

For this exercise, we've broken the time you have into three categories: professional growth, business activity and non-business activity. We'll combine them all into one statement later in this exercise.

Use your answers from the exercises above to complete the following three statements:

Non-Business Activity	The year is_____ and I am_____ *Example: The year is ____, and I am spending four contiguous weeks per year on non-business vacation-related activity. Also, I'm taking guitar lessons, am now a certified pilot and have managed to attend XX percent of my children's activities. My SO and I have averaged X date nights per month.*
Professional Growth	The year is_____ and I am____ Example: The year is _____, and I am a Vice President of Sales with 15 direct reports. I have grown myself tremendously over the last 36 months, and am certified in x, y, z.
Business Activity	The year is ____ and I am_____ Example: The year is ____ and I am spending X percent of my time, which equals X hours per week, working in a business I created and for myself. My business activities are generating $_____in revenue and annual growth rates of $_____. The business has _____employees, $_____in cash on hand and I am well positioned to acquire my competitor.

OUTCOME STATEMENT EXERCISE 4

EVALUATE YOUR RESPONSES

1	What will be different when I achieve those outcomes?
2	What will I see and feel?
3	How will I know I'm on track for achieving those outcomes?
4	What resources (team, financial, etc.) do I need to achieve those outcomes?
5	Who do I need to support me in those outcomes (employees, family, bankers, etc.)?
6	How will I know if I'm going off course?

Based on your answers to these questions (and others that may have come to mind), evaluate your three Outcome Statements and make sure they have enough detail in them.

For instance, if "four weeks" of vacation is a goal in three years, and you need an executive team to support that goal, which you currently don't have, then add: "I've hired an incredible executive team that affords me the ability to take four contiguous weeks from conducting business activities."

147

PUT IT ALL TOGETHER: YOUR OUTCOME STATEMENT

This last step combines the three category statements above into one great mash-up that is your life and how you will be spending your time three years from now.

Sample: The year is ____, and I am spending four contiguous weeks per year on non-business vacationrelated activity, stopping the business activities at 4 p.m.
on Monday – Thursday and not working at all on Fridays. Also, I'm taking guitar lessons, am now a certified pilot and have managed to attend XX percent of my children's activities. My SO and I have averaged X date nights per month. To help support those objectives, I have hired a management team, allowing me to professionally grow to the actual role of being a president who thinks strategically, rather than the taskfocused person I was three years ago. I've also become certified in x, y and z. My business activities are generating $_____in revenue and annual growth rates of $_____. The business has _____employees, $_____in cash on hand and I am well positioned to acquire my competitor.

Let's Look at What You Just Wrote

Your statement declares what your life will be like in 12 quarters and it combines work, personal and professional into one statement. You have only one bucket of time to spend, and your statement reflects this. Don't underestimate the importance of living a fused life –
now.

THIS STATEMENT MAY HAVE, FOR THE FIRST TIME IN YOUR LIFE, FUSED YOUR LIFE INTO ONE BUCKET OF TIME THAT YOU CAN SPEND. IT'S REALITY, AND NOW YOU'RE GOING TO LIVE IT.

Read your Outcome Statement every day, and your mind will start to solve the problem of how to create your life, rather than just focusing on routine and distracting tasks.

BUILD YOUR PLAN

With your Outcome Statement written, the next step is to break it down into actionable goals that must happen over the next 12 quarters.

The figure below is a presentation of the "Block Exercise," the second step in our process. We'll get to that in more detail later in the book, but I wanted to show you now how the 12 quarters are represented.

I've named each category after a similar description of the creation and evolution process that brought you and our known universe into existence. The names for Quarters 2 –

Quarter 1: The Word		
The Big Bang	2	3
The Curtain of Light	4	5
First Candles in the Darkness	6	7
Threats and Ribbons	8	9
Lights Fall On	10	11
Quarter 12: Manifested Outcome		

11 came from a display at the Griffith Observatory in Los Angeles.

The "Block Milestone Exercise" helps you evaluate your Outcome Statement through the lens of various strategic questions. You'll not only determine if your outcome is achievable but also begin the high-level process of learning how to achieve it (or adjust it if necessary).

You will first start by testing your outcome using the strategic review questions below. Then, you will create quarterly goals that need to be achieved for your 36month outcome to be realized. The boxes will help you visualize each quarter and move goals around until you have a high-level plan that is ready to be turned into a detailed quarterly plan of action with milestones (Step 3 in the planning process).

BLOCK MILESTONE EXERCISE 1

EVALUATE YOUR RESPONSES

STRATEGIC REVIEW QUESTIONS	
1	Compared to your Outcome Statement, where are you now?
2	What actionable items need to happen to get you to the 36-Month Outcome?
3	When do those actionable items need to begin for the strategic goals to be realized?
4	What could be a stretch goal, aka Big Hairy Audacious Goal (BHAG)?

BLOCK MILESTONE EXERCISE 2

EVALUATE YOUR CURRENT CAPABILITIES TO EXECUTE YOUR PLAN

Now that you have a list of action items that need to happen, let's evaluate the resources you need to execute those action items. Answers to these questions may also become quarterly goals. For example, if you determine you need to hire a team to build a product by Quarter 5, then "hiring team" will become a goal you'd place several quarters before you'd schedule the goal of completing a product.

STRATEGIC EXECUTION QUESTIONS	
1	Do I have the team in place to get me there?
2	Do I have enough cash on hand?
3	Is my current product set the right mix to reach my 3year plan?
4	What must change?
5	What's at stake if I don't hit my 36-month goal?
6	How am I positioned in the market against my competitors?
STRATEGIC EXECUTION QUESTIONS	
7	Is my USP (unique selling proposition) sustainable for 3 years or endangered?
8	Does my corporate or department structure (partners, employees, incentive plans, management, etc.) need to be adjusted?

9	What market conditions can help/hurt my progress?
10	Who do I depend on to help reach my goals?
11	BIG Question: What is the one thing I need to fix NOW to achieve my 36-month goals and what is at stake if I don't?

BLOCK MILESTONE EXERCISE 3

CREATE YOUR MILESTONES

Now that you've tested your Outcome Statement using the Strategic Review and Execution Questions above, you should have a reliable and defensible list of highlevel items that build upon each other and that need to be completed each quarter to achieve your 36-month Outcome. Those are your milestones, and we're going to prioritize them and then place them into the quarterly blocks to indicate when those milestones must be attained.

The CARVER PRIORITIZATION MATRIX

Goals can be tricky to prioritize, yet getting the right goals in the right quarters are important to meeting your outcome as planned. Don't judge yourself for having a hard time prioritizing goals. The U.S. military did, too.

153

An essential component of the military strategy is selecting the most important targets to attack. But how do you know which targets are the most important? Centuries of warfare have provided us with a reasonably intelligent answer—the CARVER Method. CARVER is an acronym for a military method of target selection: Criticality, Accessibility, Recuperability, Vulnerability, Effect and Recognizability.

The CARVER Matrix had its roots in the Vietnam War and was developed by the U.S. Special Forces as a method to rank and prioritize the targets to be destroyed. Interestingly, the matrix has now become a popular concept in business and project management. For every potential target, a value of 1 (lowest) to 5 (highest) is assigned for each CARVER factor, thereby creating the CARVER matrix. Then, by adding the six CARVER values, a total score can be calculated for each target.

These scores, when compared, produce a target prioritization list. The higher the CARVER score, the more "valuable" the target becomes.

I've adapted the CARVER method for your use. It's a fun exercise and incredibly helpful. I'd also recommend using it for team prioritization efforts as it inserts objectivity into discussions that can usually be ego-inflated and highly subjective.

CARVER Defined	
Criticality	How critical is the milestone on your organization's main objective? Will it move you significantly closer to your goal, or is it a relatively insignificant item? An example of a low-criticality goal and purpose might be building a bigger snack bar, which would be nice, but it's probably not going to make that much difference in the organization's productivity.
Accessibility	Can you hit the milestone? Or, is it so well-defended that directly attacking it is impossible?
Recuperability?	How great is the expected Recoverability and return on our commitment of resources?

Vulnerability	How vulnerable is the milestone? What amount of resources is required to hit it? Are there too many dependencies on other people or factors that may make
CARVER Defined	
	this target vulnerable to miss?
Effect	If you successfully meet the milestone, how widespread will the impact be? If you complete your goals and objectives, what effect will it have on the longevity of the organization?
Recuperability	Are your goals and objectives crystal clear or totally fuzzy? How easy is it to recognize the steps necessary to execute the goals? Have you completed this type of action before, or will you have to figure out the steps as you go along? Clear goals with clear steps will score higher on recognizability than foggy goals with unclear steps.

USING THE CARVER SYSTEM

The best way to implement CARVER is to put all your strategic goals into a spreadsheet and then score them. Let's look at this example:

	C	A	R	V	E	R	Score
Get certified	5	3	3	3	5	4	23
Hire a nanny	3	3	3	3	3	5	20

In the chart above, the two goals listed are critically analyzed and scored to determine the proper prioritization of resources. The score is close: certifications beat hiring a nanny only by three points.

Let's look at the two highest scores.

Criticality: Certifications scored as highly critical to the 12-quarter goal. Without them, the goal would be jeopardized.

Effect: The certification was determined to have a highly favorable impact on the goal.

However, to make time for the certifications, a nanny may be required. The nanny scored higher on Recognizability, meaning it is one that all stakeholders clearly identify as a need. Scores less than a five may need some internal selling to convince others that the goal is worth pursuing.

The real benefit of running goals through the CARVER matrix is that it forces you to think through each objective thoroughly. Often, we get ideas and just rush ahead with them, only to realize that the team we need to implement them didn't recognize the goal as crucial to the mission, or thought that other ideas that took fewer resources were just as capable and worthy of attention.

157

BLOCK MILESTONE EXERCISE 4

COMPLETE THE BLOCK EXERCISE

1	Place your Outcome Statement in block 12—the last quarter. This is what your life will look like in 12 quarters.
2	Place the milestones that you've prioritized in each block, working backward from block 12. This will determine when that goal needs to be started for it to be completed on time.

Example 1:
Q5 Goal—complete product A. For this to happen, the following two goals need to be listed in the corresponding quarters (boxes).

Quarter 1 goal: Hire product team.
Quarter 2 goal: Begin developing a product.

Example 2:
36-Month Outcome is to have $1 million in net profit.

Quarter 1 goal: Build a plan.
Quarter 3 goal: Finalize plan.
Quarter 4 goal: Hire a team to work plan.
Quarter 6 goal: Finish product.
Quarter 7 goal: Bring product to market.
Quarter 8 goal: Sell 10 units with $200,000 in NP.

Quarter 9 goal: Sell 10 units with $200,000 in NP.
Quarter 10 goal: Sell 10 units with $200,000 in NP.
Quarter 11 goal: Sell 10 units with $200,000 in NP. Quarter 12 goal: Sell 10 units with $200,000, achieving the goal of $1,000,000 in NP.

KEEP YOUR BLOCK EXERCISE

Military actions are generally coordinated to GPS target locations. GPS is precise, numerical and virtually error free. Your Outcome Statement is like a GPS target. It represents where you want to be—the future you are choosing to create.

Your 12-Quarter Block Exercise is the strategy you'll use to hit that GPS target. You will make many changes to your Block Exercise over the next 36 months. Don't believe for a second that life won't alter the strategy that you need to hit your target.

Whenever life tosses something at you, it places your strategy in jeopardy. Don't stress out. Pull out your Block Exercise and re-adjust.

Your target should be an inevitable part of this process. The Block Exercise is where all the action occurs.

INTERVIEW: Nancy Duarte

Nancy Duarte is the CEO and founder of Duarte, Inc., the leading firm for writing, designing and delivering compelling presentations.

159

She and her husband, Mark, originally hoped they would become pastors, but life opened different opportunities for them. They went from their tiny bedroom office doing design work to their multi-million-dollar firm focused solely on the craft of presentations. They have worked with some of the world's most respected thought leaders and brands, so the Duartes have some secrets to success under their belt.

Three of Nancy's Secrets to Success:

1. Leaders must be mature goal setters. Young leaders often approach their goals for the organization as a directive, rather than collaborative, she said. As she grew, she realized that the best goals may start with her but are honed through collaboration with her executive team. Everyone takes ownership of the vision when this happens, and together, they are accountable for achieving it.

2. Listen. Survey the employees, take listening tours and try to understand what is being felt and communicated, not just what is being said. This requires an active effort to set aside individual biases to build a culture where everyone feels heard.

3. Leaders must develop the ability to set the best course to the future. Sometimes the data might tell you to go in one direction but leadership requires a bit of counter-intuitiveness. Ultimately, she says, leaders should follow their gut and the co-created vision.

Nancy's life also didn't always unfold according to her plans. One of the most challenging experiences of her life was when Mark was diagnosed with prostate cancer.

"After discovering he had cancer, our priorities changed right away," she remembers.

Mark had always been an artist, but as the business grew, he ended up spending time in analytical roles like IT and finance. After the diagnosis, he decided to paint again. He's working on a memoir and babysits our grandson two days a week."

Nancy, like many successful leaders, realized that success comes from achieving desired outcomes and living a balanced life with intention toward achieving goals. The paradox her interview demonstrates is that while goals are necessary, to achieve the broader objectives, you must be ready to adapt them at any moment.

She and Mark redirected their personal goals to allow room to achieve their broader objectives. The only way to reach goals, she says, is to manage time. Executives must calendar their time and block out personal time on the calendar and then prioritize their work after they've established how their personal time is spent. Executives who are not calendar-driven are letting events run their lives rather than the other way around. That will never work, she says.

At times, the demands of the business did set her life out of balance, filling her with self-judgment that she "should spend more time with her children."
For the decade she was building the business and raising small children, Nancy was on a four-hour sleep cycle. Even though

she loved what she was doing, the pace wasn't sustainable. So, she hired a general manager to reduce her workload and free her to focus on
strategic efforts.

As you build your plan, consider how much of a drag you may be to your objectives. It is not easy for founders and business owners to let go and hand off crucial aspects of the business to others. It must happen for the business to grow and your life to be in the balance.

Try a Vision Board

One of the business owners I coach, Derrick Christy, told me a remarkable story. Years ago, he had created a "vision board." A vision board is simply a piece of paper or cardboard where you attach pictures of things you want to it and hang somewhere that you are sure to look at it daily.

On his dream board was a watch worth $40,000, a winery and a Tuscan villa. He looked at that vision board for years and then put it away.

A few years after putting it away, he found it. Here's his story:

"I was rummaging through my closet and found the vision board I had put together years ago. I was stunned at what I saw. On the board was a watch that was now on my wrist. Two days before finding the vision board, I had wired $1.3 million to a bank to buy a Tuscan villa out of foreclosure. On that villa is a winery."

The strategies he used to build his business and personal wealth to the necessary levels to afford the items on his vision board adjusted over the years, but the target never changed. Even after he had put the vision board aside, his mind continued to solve the problem with which he had presented it.

Isn't that remarkable? I think so.

The 12 Quarters You'll Experience

While every journey is as unique as the individual on it, there are many shared experiences along the 12-quarter journey. I've put together a 60,000-foot view of what you'll likely encounter during your 12 quarters.

THE 12 QUARTERS YOU'LL EXPERIENCE		
1	The Word	This quarter focuses on the power of the Word, changing the way your life and business occur, rules for the 12-quarter process and laws to live by. It culminates with you putting it all together and writing your Outcome Statement.
		We named it the Word because per religious traditions, a word was the catalyst for the Big Bang. In Yoga, the chant "OM" is believed to be the sound/word that God uttered to begin creation.
2 — 3	The Big Bang	Once your Outcome Statement and plan are in place, the second and third quarters are the explosion of activities that start your march toward quarter 12. Here, like just after the Big Bang, you are moving quickly, learning, adjusting and framing things in real time.

THE 12 QUARTERS YOU'LL EXPERIENCE

4 – 5	The Curtain of Light	As the universe began to expand, slightly cooler, condensed material starts to become visible against the curtain of light created by the Big Bang. During these quarters, your plan will begin to settle and to move forward will be more natural.
6 – 7	First Candles in the Darkness	400 million years after the Big Bang, gasses start to collapse and form the first lights after the explosion. These lights continue to condense and form galaxies. During these quarters, you will see many of your outcomes become or form into reality.
8 – 9	Threads and Ribbons	Dark matter shapes galaxies and creates superclusters and the largest structures of the universe. Stars and suns are formed. As we head into the last few quarters, your outcomes become more attainable and the picture you painted for quarter 12 is developing into reality.
10 – 11	Lights Full On	Galaxies were completely formed at this stage of creation. By this time, the outcome you desired should be nearly formed. There's just one quarter to go.

THE 12 QUARTERS YOU'LL EXPERIENCE

165

12	Manifested Outcome	You've made it through the first 12-quarter sprint. What you wrote in quarter 12, your Word has likely become realized in whole or in part. You've adjusted along the way, as all creation adjusts and adapts as it moves forward toward its broader goal.

EXECUTE YOUR FIRST QUARTER

John D. Rockefeller holds the title for being one of the wealthiest persons that ever roamed planet Earth. His net worth, inflation adjusted for 2016, was $392 billion (Wikipedia).

Along with that path to astronomical wealth creation, he identified some habits for success that now run the world's wealthiest corporations.

Known as the 10 Rockefeller Habits, they focus on communication, repeatability and predictability of forward motion.

My third step in the Live Fused process is based on these four Rockefeller habits:

HABIT #1: THE EXECUTIVE TEAM IS HEALTHY AND ALIGNED.

This habit applies whether or not you have an executive team. To be aligned and healthy with yourself, you need to read your Outcome Statement every day. Seriously. Every day. Doing so will align your mind with your goals and, as we've already covered, it will begin to solve them for your Outcome Statement even if you're unaware of what it is doing.

HABIT #2: BE ALIGNED WITH THE #1 THING THAT NEEDS TO BE ACCOMPLISHED.

As you move your goals from your Box Exercise to your Plan of Action and Measurement, you'll be aligning yourself with the most important things to be accomplished each quarter to forward your 12-quarter goal.

HABIT #8: YOU AND YOUR EMPLOYEES CAN ARTICULATE THE MAIN GOALS OF YOUR STRATEGIC PLAN.

With the goals ever in the forefront, you'll be able to bring them to your mind at any time. If you have accountability partners, employees or significant others who are honed into your goals and mission, make sure they know what you need to accomplish and how they can help.

HABIT #9: YOU CAN ANSWER QUANTITATIVELY WHETHER YOU HAD A GOOD QUARTER OR WEEK.

Your plan of action and measurement is designed to provide the information necessary for you to judge your progress accurately toward your goals at anytime. This is important because life and its distractions will interfere with your ability to execute your objectives. By having a system in place that makes progress toward those goals clear, you are better served to adjust when necessary to ensure completion of important items key to your 12- quarter outcomes.

THE PLAN OF ACTION AND MEASUREMENT

Once your milestones are positioned in each quarter, take two quarters and plan how to accomplish those milestone goals using the Plan of Action and Measurement (POAM) form.

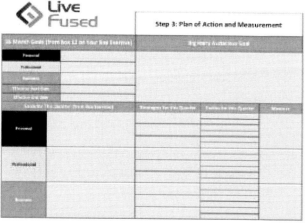

This form combines your personal, professional and business activities into one complete plan that you'll refer to at least once a week. Here's how to complete it:

1	Place your milestone goals in the "Goal" column.
2	Think about how you are going to accomplish each milestone. For instance, a goal to lose five pounds may have a strategy of hiring a trainer.
3	The tactics for hiring the trainer may require interviewing three different trainers and visiting a few gyms.
4	You'll measure your progress in the measurement column by setting dates. If you haven't interviewed three trainers by a certain date, you'll know your goal of losing five pounds may be in jeopardy.

THE SECRET OF THE POAM

Yes, it looks like a spreadsheet, but it is your plan to create the 12-quarter outcome for all your life. It is your life and business coach rolled into one document that you can follow, adjust and measure.

When marching on your path, you'll run into strategies that didn't work as you thought they would. You know there's no failure, and with your new vocabulary in hand, you'll call an "R" for redirect, write down a new strategy and keep marching forward.

As you experience life through the POAM, you'll implement the tools and ideas you've learned earlier in this book. The more you put them to use and see them come to life, the deeper embedded into your mind they will become. At some point, these ideas will be proven, and they'll become beliefs.

In other words, not only will you be building your outcome, but you'll also be transforming the way you think. And when you transform, others around you may transform as well.

TAKE IT TO YOUR REPORTS

Several executives I coach have taken the POAM, shared their business objectives with their reports and required them to complete their POAM with their targets mapping up to the overall goals set by the executive.

Each month, they review the POAM, adjust it if necessary and move forward. Teams dependent on each other have shared strategies that appear in their plans.

The fourth step is the daily accountability tracker.

DAILY ACCOUNTABILITY TRACKER

A winter's day
In a deep and dark
December,
I am alone,
Gazing from my window to the streets below On a
freshly fallen silent shroud of snow.
I have no need of friendship; friendship causes pain.
It's laughter, and it loves I disdain.

I am a rock, I am an
island.
Don't talk about love, But I've heard
the words before; It's sleeping in my
memory.
I won't disturb the slumber of feelings that have died.
If I never loved, I never would have cried.
I am a rock,
I am an island.
I have my books
And my poetry to protect me,
I am shielded in my armor,
Hiding in my room, safe within my womb.
I touch no one, and no one touches me.
I am a rock,
I am an island.
And a rock feels no pain,
And an island never cries.

We all tend to think we are rocks and islands unto ourselves.
That song by Simon and Garfunkel, in fact, has been my motto
since I was a teenager. I loved it. It struck a chord with me and
likely played a part in shaping the rather isolationist human that
I became throughout my thirties and mid-forties. Like many
people, I still battle the desire just to be alone and do things on
my own.

The truth is, however, we are not rocks, and we are not islands unto ourselves. As John Donne, the famous English poet wrote (and I paraphrase):

"NO PERSON IS AN ISLAND UNTO THEMSELVES. IF A PIECE OF DIRT BE WASHED AWAY FROM THE ISLAND, THEN ENGLAND IS LESSER FOR IT. ASK NOT FOR WHOM THE BELL TOLLS, IT TOLLS FOR YOU."

Donne is correct. Even if we believe ourselves to be isolated rocks and islands, the truth remains: we need the community to succeed.

With community comes accountability. Accountability is a fundamental component to success. My accountability partner Kris and I created a weekly tracker of the things we wanted to do daily to reach our 36-month goals.

Among those items are:

- Reading our Outcome Statements daily
- Working out 5 times per week
- Meditating daily
- Reading books together
- Spending time with the family
- Date nights with our respective SOs
- Video calls with each other
- Drinking half our body weight in ounces of water each day
- Taking vitamin supplements

We also challenged each other to "try something new" once per quarter. Our "new" seemed to have been limited to books. Although we were each completing our trackers and had visibility into each other's results, neither of us routinely checked the other's progress.

Look at the results:

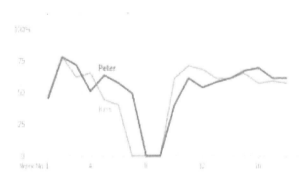

Over the 18-week period, we tracked each other closely. Kris lives 7,800 miles away from me in Hong Kong. She's 12-13 hours ahead, depending on daylight savings time. Given the separation of time and space, it is remarkable that we tracked each other to the degree that we did. The significant dip in the chart is during a time when she was traveling and I had major surgery.

Our results aren't that stellar. We're two coaches who barely held the line at a median of 60 percent completion. Yikes. After seeing this chart, we both vowed to hit at least 80 percent next time.

Another interesting byproduct of our accountability was that our production went through the roof. Before we became accountability partners, Kris averaged reading about six books per year on her own; I'd read about twelve. In the first seven months of being accountability partners, we read 10 books together. Kris read four others on her own, and I read six others on my own. I also wrote two full drafts of two new books (this one included) with Kris contributing to this one and editing the other. We did all this while she spent more time with her children when home, held a full-time job and became a certified coach and transformational leader.

For my part, I was building two businesses and coaching approximately 30 CEOs and executives, which included driving over 1,000 miles per month.

Both of us would like to say we understand fully the "why" behind this tremendous productivity increase. We didn't add time to our lives, yet together we seemed to squeeze more into the time we had while also adding a greater sense of work/life balance to the equation.

Kris, in her own words:

I'll admit it, the accountability portion of the Live Fused process left me skeptical at first. I had completed many other developmental and goal-oriented programs before, and many suggested the use of accountability partners but kept them as "optional."

I view myself as a very self-motivated person who doesn't need support to complete tasks on time, so I never bothered to engage with an accountability partner in the past. With the Live Fused process, I decided it was time to do something different than I had in the past, and I committed to being all-in. Peter and I became accountability partners, and the results speak for themselves.

After reviewing our results at the 6-month mark, I had read 2x the number books vs. the previous 12 months; I was working out and meditating much more consistently than ever before, and my husband and I had been on more date nights in the previous 3 months we had than in the prior 12 months.

I'm jubilant with the results that having an accountability partner brings. It's truly the difference between day and night. Somehow just knowing that another person is going to check in with me to see if I have done what I committed to doing provides just that extra motivation to make me do it instead of "waiting until tomorrow."

In retrospect, Peter and I could have, and likely should have been, pushing each other harder on some of our goals, and that is why our target for the next 6 months has been adjusted to 80 percent vs. the 60 percent achievement we hit over the last period.

The Power of an Ecosystem

In addition to being an executive coach, I'm also a chair on three peer boards through Vistage International. Vistage has more than 20,000 members worldwide and is considered the leading, most exclusive peer board in the country.

According to an audit of Vistage member companies by Dun & Bradstreet, Vistage companies have compound annual growth rates twice that of non-Vistage member companies.

Why is that?

Accountability and peer advice. Executives come into our boards focused on the daily tactical grind and find that within two years, they've not only been thinking strategically but have also freed themselves from the very tactics that gave the illusion of productivity while generating the chains of tyranny.

Accountability isn't for everyone. Some people prefer to remain islands and leave peer boards the moment their peers hold them accountable to their word. Their growth suffers as a result.

If a peer board isn't your style, find an excellent executive or life coach to work through your 12-quarter plan with you.

Whether you're dramatically changing your life, building a company or using this book to plan your 12quarter household goals, peers will make your experience better.

Case Study: Susan Fuller

While this system was born out of need to help business owners re-calibrate their lives, and it can work well as a life-planning platform for anyone.

After being a stay-at-home mom for 20 years, Susan was facing a major life transition back into a career. But she struggled just like most of us to chart a course of steps to reach a desired outcome.

"I liked the structure, planning guidance and direction the 12-quarter platform provided," she said. "On it, I could prepare yoga teacher certification over the course of eight months, then starting my yoga business, then getting other certifications all in a planned progression, rather than being overwhelmed by the enormity of a life transition."

She equates the process with having a tax or investment advisor.

"WE HAVE ADVISORS AND DOCTORS THAT WE USE, BUT WHY DON'T WE ASK OURSELVES WHAT WE'RE DOING REGARDING OUR LIFE ROADMAP? THIS BOOK AND PROCESS DOES JUST THAT. THIS IS A DEVELOPMENT PROGRAM. YOU'RE INVESTING IN YOURSELF."

COMMENCEMENT

Your 12 Quarters have begun, and you've already made an incredible amount of progress toward realizing the outcome you've declared into existence.

Now, you just have to do the work and let time do the rest. The road ahead isn't going to be easy. Nothing worth attaining is ever easily acquired, right? This is no different. It will take 12 quarters. And those quarters are going to fly by faster than you think.

As I mentioned before, one of my clients owned a small business with about $3 million in annual revenue, 40 percent of which came from one customer. He joined the Vistage peer board I chaired and received advice from his peer group and me to immediately—and with urgency—diversify his income.

Urgency wasn't a word in his dictionary, and he and his business partner dithered about for 18 months. Half of his 36 months were gone—just like that. And on month 19, he lost 40 percent of his revenue overnight.

His comment:

"WE JUST ASSUMED THAT OUR CUSTOMER WOULD ALWAYS BE THERE; DIVERSIFYING THE REVENUE, JUST DIDN'T SEEM TO BE A PRIORITY. I CAN'T BELIEVE IT WAS 18 MONTHS AGO WE PUT THAT ON THE PLAN." That one statement broke all the rules we've covered, didn't it? I hope you picked up on them:

1. "We just assumed"—breaks the 3rd agreement that says, "don't make assumptions."
1. "Diversifying revenue didn't occur as a priority"—the CARVER method would have changed that, for sure. The first law of performance was also in play. It didn't occur as a priority, so the action taken was not sufficient.

2. "18 months ago we put it on the plan"—there was no action or accountability, and he broke the first agreement—being true to your word.

WHAT YOU'LL FACE: BIG BANG QUARTERS

During your Big Bang quarters (2 and 3), you're likely going to launch with an explosive euphoria-backed energy. Your mind, freed from the chains of limiting beliefs that once held it in place, will be running faster than you've ever experienced.

It's important to celebrate every victory—even ones that occur "small." That's a judgment word; dismiss it. If you've managed to work out five times a week for an entire quarter for the first time in years, get excited. If you've signed up for the course that

will begin your journey to a new career, grab a glass of champagne and
offer yourself a toast.

You get the idea.

Use your new-found energy to build momentum that will carry you forward into the next quarters. Each victory is making a new case in your mind that you can achieve your goals; that which you thought was impossible is possible.

Your strongholds of limiting beliefs will begin to crumble; situations will occur differently; language will be carefully chosen and evaluated, and your life as you once knew it will start to happen as a curiosity worth remembering and not reliving.

And most importantly, you'll believe the unbelievable truth that all things are possible and the past has no correlation to the future.

WHAT YOU'LL FACE: THE CURTAIN OF LIGHT

Quarters three and four continue your explosion into the second half of your first year. By now some of your goals have been met, and many are building upon each other, and your work continues to manifest the reality you've chosen to create.

It's a beautiful, amazing scene you'll be watching and participating in as the main playwright and lead actor. There's a good chance that the second plan may start to reveal itself—the one the universe or the divine had in store for you. An event or two may have dismantled some of your goals. Perhaps your plan is only off slightly. Whatever the situation, you've remembered

179

that it is neither good nor bad; right nor wrong; success nor failure.

You've pulled out this book, re-read the first few chapters, noted the change, evaluated your responses and kept your course.

This was your first experience with the CHURP model of communication and an entire process for execution. And it feels good. You get it now, more than you did before. Experience is the best teacher, and you're an exceptional learner. Your curtain of light is beginning to unfold in your mind, casting out the shadows of doubt and rebuking old biases.

WHAT YOU'LL EXPERIENCE: FIRST CANDLES IN THE DARKNESS

I love this description; not because I'm the one who ripped it from Griffith Park, but rather because it describes life in quarters six and seven. With a year under your belt, some of the specific objectives in your Outcome Statement have likely been completely formed and realized.

It was during this period that I became the "Vistage Rookie of the Year" for my efforts at executive coaching and building peer boards. Attaining that honor was on my Outcome Statement, and I worked diligently in what Vistage considered a nearly impossible market to achieve that goal.

It was during this period that Kristina Perry who cofounded Live Fused with me, achieved her first certification and began work on her second.

Kristina Perry, In Her Own Words

I had enjoyed a very challenging and engaging corporate career, one that enabled me to travel the world and landed me living overseas on an expat assignment. As a result, I delayed motherhood until my late 30s and even had my second daughter at age 42.

After my girls had been born, I had a desire to put a plan into place which would ultimately allow me to create my work schedule so that I could spend more time with my girls. I knew I needed a concrete plan to make this transition or my dreams might remain just that – dreams.

I created my plan, spent time researching possible career avenues, decided on a path and enrolled in my first course to become a certified coach.
After this first 12-month course, I knew without a doubt that I had found a career path that both lit me up and gave back to those I coached. I decided then to up-level my training and enrolled in two additional coaching and transformational leadership courses as well as began coaching clients.

The passion and excitement I had for my new career path spilled over into my corporate life, and I was recruited to lead Asia operations for a multinational company. It might sound like a lot, but when you're following your passion and fusing your business and personal life into one, time does expand for the people and the things that you love.

———

Both of us created something tangible out of nothing but our word that manifested during these quarters. She is credentialed, and I'm recognized as a top player in my field.

181

These "wins" are important to our psyche. Before achieving them, she and I had to believe we could achieve. Neither of us had circumstances optimal to fostering such faith.

We believed, we achieved, and now the shadows of doubt that tormented us through the first seven quarters are all but forgotten. We have the mental and spiritual fuel to move forward, keep building, progressing and achieving.

And God knows we would need it in the next quarters.

WHAT YOU'LL FACE: THREADS AND RIBBONS

For some reason, life tends to make the home stretch the loneliest and longest. I can't be the only one who feels the last mile is the longest.

As you're rounding the corner with quarters eight and nine into the home stretch year, you've likely changed quite a bit. Your employees, family, and SO have probably noticed changes in your vocabulary, leadership skills and overall outlook. Perhaps you are less anxious now than before and more optimistic about your chances to achieving your outcome.

These quarters may test your limits. Part of the reason these quarters tend to be tougher than others is that the changes you made earlier are now either proving to be working or in need of course correction. Likely, it's a mixture of both. Some of your changes will be working; others may not occur that way. This is where you get creative. You aren't a quitter, and you've already proven that the concepts in this book work. You're more determined than ever to continue to put them to use and find the most ingenious solutions available to keep you on course toward your Outcome. You're surrounded by the threads and ribbons of your making and keenly aware that two plans are unfolding now and the one that isn't yours is there to prod you into an alternative path toward your stated objectives.

WHAT YOU'LL FACE: LIGHTS FULL ON

Two more quarters left. You can see the light of your Outcome Statement clearly in the distance. It's almost right there.

Perhaps you've already achieved your desired Outcome before Quarter 12. Some of my clients did just that and then realized they could have created more audacious goals. That's okay. There are another 12 quarters to go after this set is complete.

If your desired Outcome does not appear to be a few quarters away, that's okay, too. Remember, you still have until the end of the 12th quarter.

Don't let depression sink in if this is the case. There is no failure, only events that serve as our greatest teachers. Keep moving, keep creating, keep attaining. You're tough, resilient and creative. You are going to make it happen.

WHAT YOU'LL FACE: MANIFESTED OUTCOME

Congratulations! You've completed *Start with You*. You likely have many of the toys, certifications, charitable giving goals, revenue, savings and other goals you outlined three years ago in place now. Hopefully, you are doing fewer business activities, and those activities exist now only to serve your needs and not the other way around.

You're at the top of the pendulum, with business swinging all around you; but you remain steadfast and calm.

EPILOGUE

The primary purpose of this process is not to help you achieve your goals; it is to free you from yourself.

Certain principles can't be read and practiced immediately. They must be lived and absorbed into the fabric of our tissue. They must become us, and we must become them. This book is packed with such ideas. Personally, I'm still absorbing and living them. It's a daily challenge to fight the negative thoughts that trumpet through my head daily.

My ego mind is ridiculous. It forgets accomplishments almost instantly and only focuses on situations that did not arise as I expected. It judges me, accuses me and constantly bombards me with fear of failure.

And I know better.

Yes, I do.

What made me stronger and more capable of fighting these demons is experience. With experience come breakthroughs. A breakthrough is a point in time where a principle learned becomes a principle believed. And once believed, it becomes part of who we are.

I HAVE A DREAM

I have a dream that everyone in the world who struggles with a purpose left unfulfilled will free themselves through the power of many small victories and believe that nothing is impossible.

I have a dream that everyone in the world who was told they'd never achieve greatness will use this book to be their greatest self.

I have a dream that the millions of dreams now trapped and held captive by misperceptions and limiting beliefs will be freed to cure cancer, transform our transportation systems, create light speed propulsion, end war and famine and move humanity forward—always forward. Are my dreams too lofty? Anything is possible. :-)

About the Author

Peter Fuller is the CEO of Live Fused, Inc., an executive coach and board chair with Vistage International.

Before becoming an executive coach and founding Live Fused, Peter was a serial entrepreneur from Silicon Valley who helped launch 13 companies, two industry associations and one non-profit. Among these enterprises were four of his own, where he held founding-level, President, or other executive positions. During that time, he helped raise more than $60 million and participated in two successful acquisitions.

Not everything Peter has done has turned to gold. Throughout his career, he's achieved some of his goals and fallen short of reaching others. He's had to reduce his salary to keep others employed and even lay himself off from a company he founded to keep it running when venture capital money did not materialize.

"LIFE IS FULL OF TWISTS AND TURNS AND UNRAVELS MUCH LIKE ITS SOURCE CODE, DNA, LOOKS: MULTIPLE STRANDS OF EVENTS—SOME WE PLAN, OTHERS SEE HAPPEN TO US. ULTIMATELY, WE HAVE A CHOICE AND RESPONSIBILITY TO OURSELVES TO FUSE BUSINESS, PERSONAL AND COMMUNITY INTO ONE WONDERFULLY FUSED LIFE. THAT'S WHAT THIS BOOK WILL HELP YOU DO."

Recommended Reading

- *The Three Laws of Performance: Rewriting the Future of Your Organization and Your Life* by Steve Zaffron and Dave Logan
- *The Four Agreements: A Practical Guide to Personal Freedom* by Don Miguel Ruiz
- *The Law of Attraction: The Basics of the Teachings of Abraham* by Esther and Jerry Hicks
- *Essentialism: The Disciplined Pursuit of Less* by Greg McKeown

Visit Me

For resources, coaching or more information, please visit the web sites below.

www.petercfuller.net www.catipult.ai

Made in United States
North Haven, CT
08 November 2021

10956169R00111